BECAUSE I'M
SINGLE

Do Not Stir Up or Awaken Love until the Appropriate Time (Songs 8:4 HCSB)

I0109064

VISIONARY DREAMERS

EL-ROY R. COOK

BECAUSE I'M SINGLE

Unless otherwise stated, all scripture quotations are from
The Holy Bible, English Standard Version®(ESV®), copyright©
2001 by Crossway Bibles, a publishing ministry of Good News
Publishers. Used by permission. All rights reserved.

Scripture quotations identified NKJV are from the New King
James Version. Copyright 1982 by Thomas Nelson, Inc. Used
by permission. All rights reserved.

Produced by:
Visionary Dreamers
Registration Number: 2014/099200/07
1256 Plakkie Street,Toekomsrus 1759, Johannesburg,
Gauteng Province, RSA

Mobile:
083 6813 977
076 0118 411
Website: www.visionarydreamers.co.za
E-Mail: info@visionarydreamers.co.za

Printed in South Africa

ISBN:
Paperback: 978-0-620-60123-8
EBook: 978-0-620-60124-5

CONTENTS

Chapters

ENDORSEMENTS

I believe the greatest gift to give anyone is a chance to change. No one grows up with the intention of becoming a drug addict, a drop-out or a drunk, but life has a way of having its way with you. Many say it's the card you're dealt, it's your lot in life.

At some point in their life, everyone will encounter that one chance, that moment in time that has the ability to change the course of their destiny and history if heeded. It is evident in El-Roy's life today that he has seized the opportunity, to change with everything he's got and is now reaping the reward of his wise choice.

My first encounter with El-Roy was through our organisation "4Change Foundation" of which I am the founder and CEO. We had started our program in the high school El-Roy attended at the time, Randfontein Secondary School. We discovered El-Roy and his twin brother running the school with drugs, gangs and gambling.

Being a part of our programme changed El-Roy's life dramatically and these were his words: "I met them when my life's journey was at a low being involved in gangs and drug abuse; they were like a glimmer of hope inspiring and motivating me to develop a different perspective on life and made me realise that I am far more than my past or present situation. I have since matriculated and am still dreaming of greater things."

We merely provided the opportunity to change; he ultimately made the choice to change. El-Roy displays remarkable leadership abilities and qualities that have impacted the lives of many in his hometown community and now in the South African Navy too. He has the ability to inspire others with his authenticity and charismatic personality.

I believe 100% in El-Roy and his destiny; the release of his book will bring many to the realisation that despite your adverse circumstances, anything is possible and all situations are subject to Change! May you too draw inspiration from his life and work and choose to "die empty".

DR. MAXWELL HOLLAND
FOUNDER AND CEO OF THE 4CHANGE FOUNDATION
AND SENIOR PASTOR OF KINGDOM LIFE EMBASSY

I have no doubt that whatever topic El-Roy chooses to write on, it will be tackled in a manner which is refreshing and insightful to the reader. Because I'm Single is a meaty book, penned by a young man who has gone through more than many an adult twice his age. In this, his debut book, El-Roy reaches out to those dealing with issues of the heart with honesty, sincerity and a maturity that belies his age. The clarity and strength of his convictions make this book not only inspiring but challenging to all who have the pleasure of reading it.

STACEY HOLLAND
MEDIA PERSONALITY, TV PRESENTER, MC, FITNESS ENTHUSIAST & ENTREPRENEUR

As I browsed through your soon-to-be-published book I couldn't help but admire your boldness, frankness and creative way in which you express yourself. You have managed to lay bare facts and experiences of the youth that are involved in relationships. You've put on paper your life and personal experiences, as a single individual, in such a way that very few people would dare. Through this book you've managed to break new ground and unmasked the hypocrisy of those who stand before the masses but fail to say it the way is. May the survivors of failed relationships and those who have chosen to be single for a time find solace and encouragement in your excellent book. Well done, may the Lord Jesus, who lives in you, guard your destiny and provide you a soul mate at a right time.

T.J. MARA
PASTOR, CHAPLAIN & AUTHOR (SOUTH AFRICAN NAVY FLEET CHAPLAIN)

It is a proven fact that the genre of rap and rhythm and blues are influenced by the reality of broken relationships, guns, violence, sex, and scandals; all which pose a wonderful opportunity to minister to those who have felt the pains of negativity. El-Roy R. Cook in this book clearly spells out that there is another way… The Jesus Way.

REV ANDREW B.G LEWIN

DEAN OF PAT KELLY BIBLE COLLEGE

_____

We live in an ever-evolving society, from technology, to politics and even to social interactions. This has led to certain things being more accessible and more acceptable, of course. One area that has been impacted is this area called "dating". More and more young people are increasingly under pressure to find what is fondly referred to as a "life partner". With the pressures that come with that promiscuous lifestyle the extreme has become the norm where people have to experiment to settle on this life partner. This book comes as a sigh of relief to a generation that has been asking, is there not a standard? Is it no longer fashionable to be single? El-Roy R. Cook points us in that direction. The book is one that seeks to shift our priorities, as the author asks a very poignant question "Who AM I?" in one of the chapters. That question is not only confrontational because it requires of us to examine the sensitive areas of our lives, but it is also very revelatory because by answering it, the untapped potential of the single individual is unveiled. This book will challenge you to recalibrate your life God's way, enjoy reading & learning

BRANDON BAILEY
FOUNDER & LEAD PASTOR OF TELEIOS

_____

In this life of pain and rejection that we all experience in some form or other, what may seem trivial to some, may have caused others to terminate their lives.

El-Roy R. Cook has turned this tragedy into triumph and directed us to the "Balm in Gilead"

This book is highly recommended to all to help us heal the hurting and :

REMEMBER THE GREATEST LOVER WAS CELIBATE...."JESUS"

PASTOR JOHN VAN NIEKERK
FOUNDER SCHOOL OF PROPHETS
SENIOR PASTOR CITY HARVEST

_____

During my brief stay in South Africa I had the privilege of meeting El-Roy R. Cook and just by our conversations I was inspired by his life story and journey thus far. Hence, as a result of the condition of his heart, I am confident that his labour of love in this book will, without a doubt, inspire you as it provides you with the necessary insights from a man that has surely lived what he has written. So it gives me great delight as I salute you and celebrate your courage to complete this book. Thank you for the contribution you have made to our generation.

ASTELL COLLINS
C.E.O OF BD1 LEADERSHIP

FORWARD

I'll cut to the chase: Mr. El-Roy R. Cook has written a most engaging socio-religious biographical treatise which will find a ready-made audience among literate young adults and knowing parents acutely concerned with the direction and destination that their children are embarking on. It touched me because of its frankness, honesty and emotional evocation. It is a good story, going deep into the very nerve of the matter without neither any hidden Religious Pontification nor Aloofness. Mr. Cook is undoubtedly a most serious-minded young man whose spirit, mind, heart and caring love, are deeply embedded in his Faith & Obedience in the Almighty KING of Kings. His Saviour, the Christ.

DON MATTERA
AUTHOR, POET AND PLAYWRIGHT

ACKNOWLEDGMENTS

Firstly I offer my deepest gratitude and thanks to my Lord, my Saviour, for teaching me the valuable lessons and principles, and for turning my test into triumph and burden into a blessing.

To my loving mother Elian Elizabeth Stevens who reared me and has been my support, my encouragement, my inspiration and motivation from day one. To my number one competitor, biggest critique and closest friend, my twin brother Lee-Roy R. Cook for believing in me when I first told him I was going to write a book and whose presence in my life has made the journey more meaningful.

To my friends, mentors and leaders for reading my manuscript and endorsing it. The value you add to my life is unmistakable. To my confidante, dear friend and sister in Christ, Jacelyn Xenia Kok for always being so eager and willing to peruse, critique and edit my manuscript, to enhance its quality. You have been a blessing in more ways than one.

Lastly, to all of you who sent me your testimonies and for all those who contributed to the completion of this book, whether through prayer, advice and any other kind of support, you all are treasured and appreciated.

DEDICATION

I dedicate this book to all those who have ever been hurt and bitterly disappointed as a result of a failed romantic relationship. May you find clarity, comfort, healing, restoration and a renewed sense of purpose as your peruse through these pages.

To you struggling to make your current relationship work, and to all the singles, dear son and daughter, husband and wife in waiting, may you learn to pursue purpose in Christ before you pursue a partner.

INTRODUCTION

Our definition of love and dating is perverted at times. Love and romantic relationships have often been acquainted with the many wrongs, prejudices, ills and injustices manifested towards mankind.

If it's not the latest celebrity scandal, affair or divorce that the media is so quick to publicize, then it's the sitcoms, dramas and movies portraying an array of failed, dysfunctional and distorted relationships. Instead of showcasing families with strong values, morals and principles, who remain faithful, true and united, they portray the displaced and dysfunctional. Perhaps this is because there really are so few faithful families? Our views are greatly shaped by the media and the world around us and we tend to gravitate more often to that which is known, and repeatedly seen. This becomes conduct, common practice and it forms our culture. One of these practices is recreational dating, which is dating for the fun of it, or with no clear sense of purpose. There is no thought of marriage being the ultimate goal as people frantically jump from one failed relationship to the next, hoping this would be the one that would work where the others have failed. Alternatively, some of us just sabotage our own relationships in order to ensure that they do fail, as if it's all just a game.

Furthermore, with teenage pregnancy at a high, growing numbers of marriages ending up in divorce, and children being raised by single parents, one might ask, "what's the reason for this?"

Well, it is clear that we live in a promiscuous society, where we have become the instant generation, where we want what we want and we want it now! Thereby robbing us of the learning opportunity associated with patience and endurance. Where our immediate gratification has short-circuited the results of what we could have been and would have become if we had only waited and like a premature baby, the results can be rather devastating. Teenage pregnancy, high divorce rates, single parents and broken homes are the result of failed relationships. Furthermore, it is the consequence of rushing in too soon, and realizing too late the consequences of one's actions. The Bible is not kidding when it says, *Desire without knowledge is not good and whoever makes haste with his feet misses his way.* (Proverbs 19:2) Have you perhaps missed your way?

What if the only time you were allowed to date was the day you were financially stable, responsible and spiritually matured to leave and cling to what would become your new family? What if you assessed the foundation first before you began building the house and come to the place where you say, "I do"? What if dating was the most unpopular practice?

What if you shared your first kiss on your wedding day and you were patient enough to wait? It would be more magical and special, like someone opening a gift with great anticipation for the first time, it would be a love story you would be proud to tell…

Many times it is not what feels right that matters but what is right that does! Knowledge often protects us, by keeping us safe from making a premature or vital decision that can endanger our happiness or prove to be very harmful, if not lethal. I am always reminded that our decisions have a direct impact on how our lives turn out, for they influence every course, aspect, action and direction we take. Hence, every decision we make should be carefully considered.

I am also constantly aware of the stigma that is attached to being single. Due to secular doctrine we are made to believe that being single is a disdainful experience, when it should be viewed as a time to grow, learn and discover who you truly are, for it gives you that much needed time and space to put your life into perspective. You are pure, whole, and free to discover, to go and do whatever you choose. This is a season of your life to be instructed, structured and empowered by God.

So, for the hearts that were broken, all too often... for those still bitter with the wounds and scars of rejection, this book is for you. If you have ever experienced the trauma or disappointment of a failed romantic relationship and have stood shaking your head in disbelief, asking yourself, "why did it fail? I thought it would work out and this was the one" ... or maybe you haven't as yet even been in a romantic relationship ... before you rush into a relationship, learn to be patient, learn to wait and cherish your singleness, because being single is a lot wiser than being in a relationship for all the wrong reasons.

This book is not a one-size-fits-all formula, or about standard steps that says just follow steps A, B and C. Rather, it's about guidelines, about seasons, values and principles, some of which, when applied in life, could indeed prove to be fruitful and not just food for thought. Thus, while some of us are called to be single but for a season, some are called to be single for a lifetime. Every season has its beauty and significance.

In a nutshell, this book is about learning to cherish and triumph in your single years before you find companionship, for too often we strive to reach level 5, when level 1 remains unconquered.

Be moved, mesmerised, encouraged and inspired by the insights, stories and testimonies within the book, pure edification! I pray that this book will minister to you, because it's a message that God has impressed upon my heart and first ministered to me.

CHAPTER 1

REASON FOR MY VIEWPOINT

Before a doctor can give a prescription, recommendation or perform surgery, he first has to identify or diagnose the problem. Well I'm not a doctor, but I am a patient with a problem…

BECAUSE I'M SINGLE…

It's been almost three years now since I was just about to leave home and begin my basic military training. Everything was fine then; basic training was something to look forward to, a fresh start and a new chapter of my life. Who knew, however, that life would present me with so many new starts at each bend and turn. Some came like a flood all at once, some pleasant, some not so pleasant, but I guess it's all part and parcel of this journey we call life. Change, whether we like it or not, will force itself on us, and impose its rule. At times it wrestles one into submission, the whisper of the constant reminder "things will never be the same again…" even though we sometimes long for what was and how it was.

Well back to my story, I was anxious, nervous, fearful and also filled with much joy and excitement for what was awaiting me. It was as if destiny was calling, it was something I had been waiting for my entire life and it was busy unfolding. At Johannesburg station, the place was buzzing and filled to the brim, other recruits were there too with their friends and family coming to see them off. As the time drew near, the engine of the train started warming up for our departure. I said my final goodbyes to my family and friends. As I embraced my mom to hug and kiss her goodbye, she became teary eyed and I did my best to assure her that everything was going to be okay. I tried my best to compose myself, to stay strong for them, but couldn't help being overcome with tears too; the moment was just so overwhelming. I quickly wiped them away and pulled myself together. I was going to be a soldier/sailor, so I had to man up. There was one lady who was not there, to whom I had grown attached and it was not my mom, for she was present. Her name was Jasmine; she was seventeen years old, five feet tall. She had silky, black, curly hair and brown eyes; her amber complexion reminded me of finely ground cinnamon on pancakes, which I loved.

At times she wore glasses which made her look kind of sophisticated. She was very energetic, always buzzing like a bee with an athlete's body to top it off! I felt like the luckiest guy alive to have her as my own. I often wondered what exactly I liked about her the most - was it her smile that lit up the whole room, warm and always inviting as she was so dear to me? Was it her pleasant conversation, good sense of humour and the sparkle in her eye like the radiant glow of a star shining brighter even in the darkest of night? Was it because she was good with kids and handy around the house or perhaps her laughter; she always knew just what to say and could cheer me up; there was never a dull moment when she was around. I had longed to see her and to be with her but she was on vacation with her mother and I wished she would have returned to see me off and say goodbye before my departure, but she was absent.

Nevertheless, the moment had finally dawned, the moment I was hoping for, had dreamed about, the moment often prayed for and the moment I thought wouldn't actually materialize because of the long wait, that moment had become tangible, had become real; it had at long last arrived! As I proceeded with my luggage in hand, my family and friends had their eyes fixed on me, and the military police were directing us to ensure all our documents were in order. I then climbed aboard the train, turned around and waved goodbye one last time.

The train departed from Johannesburg station late afternoon; I was on board train destiny. To serve my country with pride, dignity, integrity, loyalty and honour, I would fly the flag of the SA Navy high. This was the ethos I would abide by. There were a lot of rumours, myths and fables people had told me about the Navy prior to my departure; I was ready and eager to test the validity of those claims.

My ride on the train was a journey to savour, a journey to enjoy and remember. It was my first time travelling such a long distance by train and it would be my first time in Cape Town, our final destination. On board the train I was seated next to Jandrea. He was about the same height as me, seventeen years of age and also from Johannesburg. We quickly got acquainted, shared our snacks and I formed a new relationship, he was my first friend there. Young people like me came from all over the country, for one reason - to serve their country. I considered it such a privilege and honour to be part of the ones chosen and selected out of so many applicants. I had been trying for almost two years to get into the SA Navy and when it seemed all hope was lost and I would never be accepted, I received my acceptance letter, my breakthrough! I was exhilarated. Family and friends were overjoyed and excited for me, but none more than I was. On board the train I met new people and also formed new relationships with those who would be my comrades, my brothers and sisters in arms.

It was a three day journey, during which we were delayed a couple of times at one or two stations, whereby we would be given time to run to the shops for refreshments. Although the time we were given was limited we would explore our surroundings, we were young and adventurous. The instructors would also order us to stand in squads where we were to do push-ups and other drills, giving us a foretaste, a preview, of the rough times ahead. We finally reached Cape Town, my first time being in a place that I had always heard people talk about with such high esteem and fondness. A city famous for its beautiful scenery and one of the Seven Wonders of the World, the timeless Table Mountain now declared a World Heritage site.

My first glance of Table Mountain was magical and memorable; I saw it on the bus from Cape Town to Saldanha; a cloud covered it almost as if a table cloth had wrapped itself around it, as if God was busy preparing a feast, with creation being His guest, a sight that I marvelled at. We finally arrived at the naval base which became my home for the next six months until completion of my basic military training. This is the induction phase of every sailor or soldier, it is compulsory to complete basic training before one can go further and specialise in other careers in the Defence Force. This is also strenuous training that would either break some and they would give up and quit, or build some, as they progress and finish and come out stronger as a result of having undergone basic military training.

The first couple of days we were taken on tours to get ourselves acquainted with the base and its surroundings, including administration matters. The instructors were harsh and fierce; to make us 'wanna-be' soldiers aware that we were not at home, that this is boot camp! It was on the third day there that it happened. I had just finished watching the news, walking out of the television room and as I proceeded down the passage way towards our dormitory I received a call. It was her… Jasmine!

We had been dating for almost a month, but to me it felt like years. If you would say we were going too fast, I would tell you, "we were speeding!" She was my first official girlfriend since I had become born-again, and accepted Christ as my personal Lord and Saviour. She had also recently committed to choose Christ and live for Him. We both attended the same church, plus her mother liked me and approved of us. Things were not only looking good, but you could say going smoothly. However, communication between us started getting less and less as the days went by; the more we were apart, the more we grew apart. She was having doubts; I was having doubts, about whether or not this long distance relationship would work. We had talked about it a while back when I first received news that I would leave and had both agreed it would work out. Soon after that we started having arguments and fights over petty issues however. Still I didn't expect that she would end it that evening when she phoned me and said "it's over!" She gave me many reasons why we had to break up and I gave her even more for why she must stay. Partly, she believed I had cheated on her with her cousin. I had flirted, yes, and it had come close, but the past burned in my memory and I couldn't do it. Jasmine would hear none of it, her mind was made up and she had already moved on. She dropped the phone and then it started to sink in.

She had left me… She, the one I finally believed that I had found out of so many, the one who my restless heart would find comfort in and cease its endless wondering. I had thought my search was over when I found her. I would not let it show, I would not in so many words let her know the way I felt, but deep down I was shattered, I was heartbroken.

"Oh no! I can't believe it, not this again!" were my immediate thoughts. I had decided to be right by doing right, to stay true by her side, but how could things go so terribly wrong?

"Was it karma?" I thought, as a million thoughts started surging through my head in search of answers… "Was this what I got for all the girls I had mistreated, used and abused?" A cold dagger had pierced my heart, it was just a bad dream, at least that is what I thought and that I would soon awaken from my deep slumber, but it was not, I was wide awake and she was still gone.

Normally I would not have been so fazed by a break up; at least, that was my frame of mind about two years ago. This time it was different however; this time it hit me hard…

OPENING PANDORA'S BOX!

I was raised by a single parent, and received little guidance other than "don't have sex", which my mom would not even say in so many words. Romantic relationships were not something I would talk about with my mom, but with my friends often. And although my mom had every intention to instil strong values and rear me well, the choice of whether or not I would use them as guiding principles, as a road map to live a life of responsibility, honour and integrity, was up to me to make. There were some questions that remained unanswered, such as how to treat the opposite sex, what makes a successful romantic relationship, the dos and the don'ts, the when's and the how's and many other questions…

I began dating from an early age and at first it was as innocent as holding hands, hugs and a kiss on the cheeks as we progressed. One evening, while I was at my friend's house, the space we occupied was scarcely big enough to room the single car it was built for. Although poorly ventilated and not that tidy, it was nevertheless more like paradise to us. I would sleep over there at times. We would play games and smoke weed among other things. It was our space, our own place and our secret little hide out.We called it, "The Candy Shop." My friends suggested that I try masturbating; my friends had done it often and spoke about it so causally. At first it was strange, it was new to me. I decided to give it a try however. It was like opening Pandora's Box, an affair with lust had started which would later form a stronghold and become an addiction. My mind became polluted with the wrong images of girls, which caused me to devalue their worth. I had values, but they were misplaced at this time.

> **Values are what colour our world, they define what is important to us and what is not, we will fight or even kill at times, for what we value the most.**

Gambling, partying, alcohol, drugs and sex had become the standard practice I conformed to and I was in search of pleasure more than purpose.

I would go clubbing, attend house parties and go to different communities with friends. Our strongest pursuit was not so much the parties, alcohol or drugs, rather it was the girls.

I became a 'player'. The practice was to "date as many girls as you can, more than one at the same time, talk about it and laugh about it afterwards with the guys. Date a girl with the sole intention to have sex with her, and once you have, there is no real reason to stay any longer."

> It's like having sex was the only goal, instead of getting married and building a home, with love, loyalty, purity and patience as the foundation.

But to me all of those things were irrelevant. It was an aimless game; I used, abused and betrayed these women's trust. I would date two or three at the same time, as long as the others didn't find out about each other and when it ended I would later forget about them, as they became just a bunch of nameless faces to me.

Although I sometimes regretted that some of the relationships had ended, how they ended, it still wasn't enough to persuade me to change my ways.

A CHANGE OF HEART

I was in my last year of high school, when I became born again and accepted Christ as my personal Lord and Saviour. God started working in my heart; the heart which all the issues of life flow from, the fire of our passion and desires.

I already had a girlfriend at the time I became born-again.Her name was Nicole; she was a light, golden caramel, charming with an exquisite figure, and she disarmed me the first time I laid eyes on her. She moved as if though time had slowed down; her aroma could wake me up from a coma and all I knew is that I wanted to be with her. She had had a boyfriend when I first met her, but I had pursued her nevertheless, as I was eager to make my introduction to her known and even told her boyfriend about my intentions. I was cocky and confident. All the guys couldn't help but take note of her, her presence demanded attention, though she was gracious in manner and soft spoken. I cherished her, but most of the time while I was dating her, it was as if I just wanted to uncover her. We almost got intimate, although she always halted it and told me she was not ready for it.

Now I had become born again and although I wanted this relationship to work between me and her, I somehow knew that the relationship would end. I told her about my conversion and at first she was not sure what to make of it and I wasn't either. We tried to make it work but we shared two opposing world views. About three days after I told her, the relationship was over. I moved on and was at peace with it.

> **As I became more and more acquainted with my Redeemer, Christ, I became more and more aware of His righteousness and my own wretchedness.**

I started to have feelings of remorse and shame for the way I had treated girls in the past. I stopped dating, not by choice but because I was still finding out whom I truly was in Christ. Although I was saved, I still flirted with girls on occasion.

I then went on a church camp. I had originally gone there with impure thoughts, hoping that I would meet some beautiful Christian females, but what I received there was the cure and a real eye opener that made me ponder deeply on the way I viewed romantic relationships.

The first evening was a gala dinner with my leaders; the setting was magical, the food was delicious and the program enlightening. The leaders shared the stories of their own romantic relationships -there were three couples and they sat in the centre. The tables and chairs were all packed around them in a semi-square like form.

1. The first story I heard, was about Ron and Sherell. They had both come to church and became born again, but they were still living together. When Ron approached his pastor, to let him know that he would like to get married

to Sherell and wanted the pastor's blessing, the pastor told them that they should first learn to live apart and pursue purity and align themselves with God's will for their lives. For if God's standards are honoured God's blessings will follow. They both agreed, and in the end they got married.

2. The second story was about Ashton and Kaylen. Ashton had met Kaylen through his Mom; they both served God and loved the Lord. Ashton had still been a virgin and never really had a serious relationship, Kaylen too. Guess you could say God was preparing them to wait for each other; they got married while still being virgins.

3. The third story was about Mark and Laura. Mark was the pastor's son and engaged to Laura. They were both still virgins, and were determined to keep it that way until they got married. They finally got married having stayed true and lived up to that promise. They had understood the value of patience and the wait was worth it. They had respected each other enough, by honouring God and honouring each other.

These testimonies the leaders shared struck a chord deep within me. I was shocked and couldn't believe such things existed, in this lust-centred world - "They got married while still being virgins!?" I had been so desensitized that that which should appear normal to me appeared abnormal. It started to convict me of the system I had grown enslaved to. God was busy working in my heart, renewing my mind and performing surgery.

So the camp really had a life changing impact on my life, and it was one of the reasons I was committed to make sure my next relationship would not end up like my previous other relationships. Unfortunately when the break with Jasmine happened, it took me back and forward thinking, **"Is there something wrong with me, is there no end to this dating and breaking up story?" For when this relationship ended while I was born again, it hit me hard. I expected things to be so much more different. For if Christ was the foundation surely it should have lasted or was it just lust? What was wrong, did I not learn from past mistakes?**

I remember the excitement of having more than one girlfriend, the thrill of the relationships and intimacy I had shared with them, acting as if I had had a deep affection for them, but it was all just infatuation. Now all of that didn't appeal to me anymore. "Is God busy peeling of the layers of bondage, wrong ideas and mistaken beliefs?" I wondered...

> **I tried to make sense of the constant, endless cycle but all I knew was that this was the last straw, I had had it!**

Shortly after the break up with Jasmine, a close friend suggested a book titled, *I Kissed Dating Good Bye* written by Joshua Harris. When I finally read it, it ministered to me a profound message of pursuing God and His purpose first before anything else and truly allowing Him to be a lamp unto my feet, guiding and leading me in every avenue and aspect of my life, especially with regard to romantic relationships. It made me stop trying to persuade Jasmine, stop pursuing girls and start pursuing God´s purpose for my life first. I also decided to do just as the book suggested, to "kiss dating goodbye".

The testimonies and the book I read and every other book afterwards, were almost working like a chisel God was using, getting rid of the wrong views of romantic relationships, so that they were replaced with a God-centred view.

> **Have you found out what God wants for you or what He wants you to look for when it comes to romantic relationship or are you so busy trying to find that perfect match that you have abandoned the will of God for your life in the process? Being like Samson chasing after a Delilah?**

THE END OF THE SCAVENGER HUNT

In the wake of this last break up with Jasmine, I decided to yield my will and surrender to God's will for my life. **I started to realize that there must be more to life than just finding 'that' person and starting a family. For, if love or finding 'that' person was the destination, most people would have been there or are on their way. However, success in life is measured by whether or not they have found 'that' person, instead of whether or not they have found their purpose.**

It's no wonder it seems that everybody is on a scavenger hunt, on high alert and constantly looking around. Getting involved in a romantic relationship as quickly as possible seems to be the order of the day and the ultimate goal in life. Subsequently, if what you have found ends up in failure, the hunt continues.

We so want to be loved deeply and experience the intimacy of two people passionately in love. It is what defines our existence. "If I don't have him or her" is what we think, "I feel out, alone and I am incomplete, with my life being meaningless." So we lower our standards, sell ourselves short, engage in frivolous pursuits all for the pleasure and we hardly notice our life deteriorating.

For far too long I, too, have been on this scavenger hunt. I had thought I was making headway; it was almost as if I owned it, only to come to the sad awakening that in fact I had got it all twisted right from the start and it owned me!

I had a problem and the string of failed relationships was not the cause of the problem; merely an indication of the result of the problem. I never admitted it; I never truly realised or accepted that I had one. And because it was out of sight, tucked away and out of mind, I never acknowledged it was there. Yet it clearly lingered on and now it had arrested me with the cold hard fact, that I had taken so many steps yet it felt like I was at the same place, stuck with the same problem.

How many of you feel the same way; that after so many failed romantic relationships you are ready to give up and walk away, that you believe that you will never find your own happy ending and live happily ever after, and remaining incomplete is the assumption. We move in and out of relationships, losing ourselves, exchanging our innocence for a lie and short-lived pleasures intensifying our hunger for more. As we treat romantic relationships as mundane, robbing us of the magic such a discovery should be like, we sell ourselves to the scavenger hunt.

BECAUSE I AM SINGLE

How sad it is, that most of what we know and which defines our views and casual approach to romantic relationships is either what we have seen being portrayed by the media, or our parents who maybe even failed to make a romantic relationship work; the commitment they made may have ended up in divorce. It is not that they cannot teach us anything, however, because we learn as much from the failures of others as we do their victories. We just have to think twice before using the same mould that didn't work. Maybe even our friends try to teach us the A, B and C's of what makes a romantic relationship work, but they too have the same warped view as you and I, and are still struggling with their current romantic relationship or are on the scavenger hunt. When they invite you to join them on the hunt, it doesn't seem odd because then you will be 'in with the crowd'. "It's what everybody does, its normal, so why not me too?" is what you think.

> You see I was done appointing blame; it was time for me to man up and own up to the responsibility that I had a problem. As much as I could try and say, "well this last relationship with Jasmine ended and it was all her fault!" it would not solve anything for I was as much to blame as she was for the way things turned out. No it was time to face the man in the mirror.

I had lived my life governed by my flesh, by what feels right, too often making decisions on impulse without thinking twice about them; I was selfish and inconsiderate. I had defined being in a relationship and with someone as being the ultimate goal and thought that it would bring me completeness. To finish school, study and most importantly finding my identity and purpose was secondary, but finding that person, to be in a romantic relationship had become my prime objective. I had given in to another lie - that companionship will bring completeness - and in doing so I was expecting too much from someone else that they could never fulfil and my life still felt void. No, I had to find my completeness in Him first and my chosen partner also had too, for then we would be two complete people complementing each other one day.

> In cross questioning my whole approach to romantic relationships I decided to wait, I decided to pause before I jump frantically like I usually did, from one failed relationship to the next. For, the peril of doing the same thing over and over again and expecting a different result, is like running around in circles believing you are making progress. Like a dog chasing its tail.

Therefore, I firmly reject the claim that you have to date as many people as you can in order to be better prepared or more experienced for marriage. For what does a string of failed relationships teach you about lifelong commitment? How we live our lives as singles will shape and define how we treat our partners in romantic relationships. For by the life you are cultivating as a single, you are either learning how to cherish commitment or dishonour it, before you step into companionship. Hence, I have ended my scavenger hunt.

Above all Christ needs to be the centre that binds two people together like a three-fold rope; making it lasting, because of the everlasting covenant both have found in Him. I learned that for this to take place, I need to be prepared. The love I have for the woman in my future I will not give to another -because I am not trying, I am buying.

I am a patient with a problem; I'm being purged, processed and purified. My purpose and my steps are being ordered by my Maker…

Because I'm single…

I am single by choice, revelation and conviction.

Because I'm single, I don't have to fear being single or alone, for my attentions are made clear, I am waiting not dating.

Because I'm single, I will not succumb to peer pressure and give in to frivolous pursuits or short term pleasures.

Because I'm single, I have therefore implemented measures and precautions to ensure that the integrity of my singleness is not compromised.

Because I'm single, I will patiently wait for her; I will prepare, plan and pray for her.

Because I'm single, I will pursue virtue, purity and righteousness while protecting the sanctity of what would be, long before we come to the place where we say, "I do".

Because I'm single, I will allow God to fortify my character, renewing my mind and continuing to change my heart.

Because I'm single, I will not wallow or moan, but understand it's a season and I am greatly privileged to have God prepare me on my own for my wife to be if He so chooses.

Because I'm single, doesn't mean my life is at a pause, but rather that to You my Redeemer I am all Yours, while You guide and lead me purposely.

Because I'm single, so that I may be ready for her in my mind, body, soul and spirit, to be whole for her.

Because I'm single, I trust in His perfect timing, as I wait patiently for Him to reveal my Eve one day just like Adam, in season and under the right circumstances.

Because I'm single, I will lean not on my own understanding but in all my ways acknowledge Him and He will direct my path.

Because I am single, I will wait for a woman of God, a woman of passion, strong conviction and compassion.

A woman of courage like Deborah.

A woman of persistent, fervent prayer like Hannah.

A humble submissive woman like Sarah.

A faithful and loyal woman like Ruth.

A woman who has been purged and processed through the refinery of His word, a woman of substance, a woman for a time such as this like Esther.

She would be dressed in robes of righteousness; she would be woman like no other, she is a queen.

Because I'm single, I will therefore learn to think like, talk like, walk like and act like a king until my queen is presented to me.

Because I'm single, I do not advocate being single as the destination, but rather to wait before you date for all the wrong reasons and have you questioning afterwards "what have I become or gotten myself into?" when you find out he or she wasn't really that into you.

Because I'm single I choose not to awaken love until it's time, because love is such a powerful force, at the right time it's ripe and beautiful and when not it can be devastating.

Because I'm single, I trust that you are preparing me and her, to be suitable for each other by design, make-up, through every fabric of our being. To fit as two hands interlock, synchronized in perfect harmony, united to fit. A match made in heaven. She will be bone of my bone, and flesh of my flesh.

Because I'm single, I will not compromise to settle for less than what God has purposed for me and give into loneliness, desires, lust and all the things that seek to derail or take me away from God's original plan for us.

Because I'm single, I consider this as vital training and how I treat the ladies that come into my life is a reflection of how I will treat her, so I'll be the brother, stand guard over and cover them.

"Because I'm single" is just another season of my life and while I am there I have to make the most of it!

CHAPTER 2

WHO AM I?

Who am I? This is a frightening question because our society doesn't allow us to discover who we are. When searching for our identity we are faced with our culture, the social pressure of trying to fit in, the world wanting to make you into who they think you are or should be. But who are you really?

Some relationships are doomed before they have even started; just the denial of that reality, clouded by infatuation delays the inevitable. **Why is it doomed? - Because people do not know who they are. Think about it, how many times have you desperately tried to make a relationship work only to have it fail dismally not realizing you are the one who needed some work?**

What you believe about yourself matters. **Hence knowing oneself, knowing who you are is paramount. For we invite someone into our life on the premise of who we perceive and believe we are.** For example you will pursue someone to date, just for pleasure, sex and fun, nothing more, nothing less or for the purpose of marriage being the ultimate goal. Dr. Myles Munroe was quite right when he said, *"Man's greatest ignorance is of himself. What you believe about yourself creates your world. No human can live beyond the limits of his or her beliefs. The pattern of your behaviour is all a result of your belief system".*[1] So in order to change certain practices in your life, why you do things a certain way, it only makes sense that you should start by investigating that very belief system.

Have you ever paused to ask yourself the questions? Who am I? What on earth am I here for? What's my purpose, my identity or my destination? Our lives can become so cluttered with the maze of activities we find ourselves wrapped in, that we become frustrated that life is not working out and it becomes difficult to ask, much less find answers to these questions.

But who are you? Who are you really besides the romantic relationships you are constantly pursuing? Who are you besides the next party, clubbing, excitement and adventure you are constantly rushing to? Who are you besides your friends, who are you besides the makeup and the many add-ons of life? I am talking about the real you, the face in the mirror.

[1] Munroe, Dr. M. 2005. *The Spirit of Leadership.* United States of America: Whitaker House (pg. 17.)

When all is said and done, when the partying has stopped, the music has faded and you are left alone, does it dawn upon you, clear as the light of day, that you are certain who you are? Or has a romantic relationship become the sum of who you are?

Don't let being with someone become your full-time job, rather get one. Get a career, discover your purpose. **Romantic relationships are a chapter in your life and should not be seen as the whole book. Balance your life by discovering who you are.**

BEING SINGLE MAKES DISCOVERING WHO YOU ARE MUCH SIMPLER.

SELF-DISCOVERY BEFORE OTHER-DISCOVERY

The advantages of being single are that you can come to terms with and realize who you truly are. It allows self-discovery before the discovery of your significant other.

As we are constantly growing and learning, we will never know ourselves completely. However, before you step into a relationship, get acquainted with who you are and what your ambitions are. Do you have any dreams, or aspirations? Have you planned ahead? Are you the kind of person that will be a delight for the next person to be with? Have you planned for them and a family? Planning and knowing what it is that you are seeking out of life saves you a lot of unnecessary heartache later, when you may find yourself trying to be in a relationship and live as though you were single, because you never explored and took advantage of your single years. This creates problems and can cause the other person to feel neglected. **How sad it is when I hear married couples telling me how they wish they had maximized on their single years more, but now they are married, their lifelong dream has been realized only to become a nightmare.** Married people often try to be superman or superwoman but find the added responsibilities make this nigh on impossible. Marriage is added weight and responsibility. And you cannot be married yet also have a deep desire to live your life as a single person.

Self-discovery affords you the opportunity for sure footing and firm resolve, so that when you have the right motives, being married is the goal, not just odds flings, hook-ups and one night stands here and there. Also, when you have the right beliefs it is easy to detect and determine whether or not you have found the right person in accord with those beliefs and values you stand for when you cross their path.

You then quickly realize you don't have to drop your standards, but maintain them. When you do not know who you are, you are constantly trying to change others with the notion that each problem that arises must lie with them. Or you accept harsh treatment such as physical or emotional abuse, and stay in toxic relationships that add little or no value. All because you have this crazy idea that it's the best you will ever find, for fear that you are unworthy to be loved by another or don't deserve to be treated better.

> Self-discovery also allows you the chance to come to terms with and accept your differences. You are different; when you accept your differences and uniqueness you will give others the freedom to be different to you, instead of constantly trying to make them who you are. You can't change people but only influence them.

Have you discovered who you are, your identity and your purpose?

For a long time I also didn't know what my purpose was. My life had no purpose or rather my purpose was to sleep around so I could add the next girl to my list and how I did it was irrelevant. Things have turned for the worse and a lot of young guys and ladies are what I was like back then. There is no conscious purpose and, remember, where a principle like purpose is missing, it's replaced by something else... In this case a quick fix resulting in irresponsible actions. Thus a lot of misconceptions and insecurities are a result of not knowing who you are. Your purpose is not to be in such relationships that are only for your detriment instead of your benefit, your purpose is to add value and bring more meaning to your life as well as others'.

CONFRONTING OUR IDENTITY CRISIS

What makes us put down, mistreat and make fun of others because they don't resemble us in whatever shape, size or form? We measure their weakness on the basis of our strengths and we find more satisfaction in highlighting their problems, instead of offering a solution or examining ourselves. It's because we don't know who we are, that it is much easier to find fault in the way others are.

We don't know what to do with our lives, we don't know what we want to become and we certainly don't know who we are. With so many uncertainties, isn't it a wonder why we have so many insecurities? **Insecurities can make us vulnerable and gullible. Vulnerable and open to influences that could bring with it perils unknown, gullible to fall prey to them and become victim or perpetrator, because who we are is unknown.**

Growing up, Mike had a very serious acne problem, with pimples around his nose and upper cheeks…As he grew older, blackheads and scaring shaped the young man's face…Almost everywhere he went prejudice followed, making it difficult for him to make friends. Each morning he would wish for smoother, clearer skin, when another pimple was discovered next to one of the previous day…

Maybe you have often found yourself in a similar position, and because of your appearance or whatever affliction you have, experienced prejudice, rejection and neglect. **It's a struggle to feel any sense of worth, when no one ever tells you, you are beautiful and loved, or instils in you a sense of belonging. Thus singleness is made even more unbearable, as you just want to escape your singleness, in the hope that companionship could appease and quench your feelings of loneliness along with the other insecurities you harbour. The lengths you could go to for companionship are great.**

As a result, we want to be in a relationship because we seek security, fulfilment, we believe our completeness must be attached to another. Sadly, in companionship one gets easily discouraged as we realize this is not the case, because people place false, unattainable standards on each other, hoping that the person would be able to define their being. **Dating doesn't bring or offer any sense of fulfilment, or**

security. It may offer it in the short term but in the long run it fades. If it brought any sense of lasting security or fulfilment, why are so many people unhappy in marriages? Why is the divorce rate so high? Why do people casually jump from one failed relationship to the next? **Marriage or being in any relationship will not eliminate the problems you have; but many times it will only escalate them and make things worse.**

Inside every man and woman, there is a little boy or girl who wants to be beautiful. But who said beauty has everything to do with the exterior? However, like Mike, it is what we often accept, as this lie is perpetuated by the media.

> Everyone has flaws and defects and when we realize this, we will also realize that everyone is beautiful in their own special way. As it is often asserted that, "beauty is in the eye of the beholder", we will also realize that you are beautiful beyond compare to the person and heart that is meant to love you.

There is nothing wrong with wanting to feel and look beautiful, because in a perverted society we are often faced with the question of whether we are beautiful. You must remember this: **when God thought about something beautiful, He made you. The world never expected you, that is why the world often has difficulty accepting you.**

Whether we struggle with our appearance, acceptance, weight issues, or have been molested, hurt and abused from an early age; whether they are physical or emotional wounds caused by others or ourselves, they leave deep scaring, a blow to our self-confidence, causing us to doubt who we are and leaving an inner, ongoing battle for identity.

"You are not good enough!", "You don't fit in!", "You are a loser!", "No one loves you!", "You will never make it!" and "You are not beautiful!" Words like these pierce us deeply, reinforcing the anxieties and insecurities we have about ourselves. We all have insecurities that we have to deal with, enforced by the society and constant peer pressure. **The crisis in our societies can therefore be traced to a crisis in the home, the family, relationships, and the crisis in the individual. And because we are insecure and unsure of whom we are inside, like a wrecking ball we at times bring havoc to the world outside.** Homes are torn apart; hearts are broken, leaving the carnage of our mess because of our identity crisis.

RESULTS OF IDENTITY CRISES

- Insecurities. Insecurities cause us to be jealous, prejudicial, envious, prideful, and hateful towards others and also towards ourselves

- Lack of patience. We get our priorities twisted, as getting into a relationship takes precedence above everything else and we rush into relationships to try find meaning within ourselves.

- It causes us to foster bad habits, drugs, partying, and pre-marital sex. Sex is beautiful in the confines of marriage and outside its confines it can be destructive. Hollywood is constantly portraying that it is okay to have sex while you date, or even to officialise the fact that you are seeing each other or even worse just casually having sex randomly with whomever, whenever. You don't realize that you cannot constantly give of yourself sexually, carelessly, without reservation and expect not to be affected. For every natural act, there is a spiritual consequence as much as there are natural consequences. It may result in unwanted pregnancy, leaving a shadow of shame and guilt that the girl and boy have to deal with. Also in many instances, you find that the dad is not as committed to taking care of the baby as he was in sleeping with the girl.

- When we don't know who we are, we start to resent being single, because we say stuff like, "our biological clock is ticking" out of fear and worry that we will end up not getting the right person. **Fear paralyses our faith, brings worry and stress causing us to stop trusting in God.**

Amidst our identity crisis, we can rise up with courage to confront it, by admitting and coming to terms with the fact that we have a problem, and for every problem there is a solution, for the solution is never isolated from the problem. If we have a deep desire and willingness to search long and hard enough for a solution, we will be able to confront and triumph over our identity crises and forever break the cycle of dysfunction in our lives.

BREAKING THE CYCLE OF DYSFUNCTION

If you keep on doing what everyone else is doing you will probably end up with the same results everyone else is having -such as a string of failed relationships, a broken heart, pregnancy, abortions, divorce etc.

JUSTIN

In his final year of high school Justin attended a church camp with the intent of meeting loads of beautiful girls his age, unknowing that this retreat would change his life forever.

It was mid-year July, just after the prelims had ended, timing was excellent. That weekend at the camp, after completely opening himself for everyone to see his hurt, his pain, growing up without a dad, in an emotional packed hall where the pastor was ministering that night, he decided to give his heart to the Lord, letting go of the past, the bitterness, the un-forgiveness and hardness. When he got home, he thought that he had completely overcome his strongholds and lustful natures and broken the cycle of dysfunction pertaining to romantic relationships in his life. However his views on dating remained unchanged.

When he was younger, he and a few friends would often go on adventures at a nearby dumping site, to collect some 'treasure', as they would call it, as they say, "one man's trash is another man's treasure". They stumbled upon pornographic magazines and browsed through them. Eventually, it led to a habit of watching pornography videos and by the age of fifteen he was addicted to it. By then he had started dating, at times three different girls at once. No one had ever found out about the other. That was until it was too late. See, he wasn't in it because he saw a long-term union between two individuals, but simply to get out what he wanted and that was sex. As soon as he got it, he would conjure up another excuse to breakup with the girl in particular. He somehow knew it was wrong; still he could not be persuaded to do otherwise.

However, the true nature of his actions was being revealed in the lives of the girls whose trust he betrayed and purity he had stolen, while in search of his own fulfilment.

When he became born again, he had much remorse and guilt for what he had done and how recklessly he had lived his life, like a ship steering off course heading for a rocky shore. He especially felt shame for the way he had treated girls. He decided to stop preying on girls and not make another one a victim. A year passed and it seemed that he had outgrown that stage in his life and was making progress. That was until he met Marry-Ann.

They met through a mutual friend, Donna. Marry-Ann and Justin quickly struck up a conversation and naturally felt at ease with each other, as if they had known each other for a while. Marry-Ann was a very attractive girl, aged seventeen, with an animated personality. That night while Justin was lying in his bed, preparing to go to sleep, he found himself thinking about her. The next day he decided to get her number from Donna, because Marry-Ann lived in another town, and was only visiting and had gone back home already. After he received her number, Justin then called her; she was surprised to hear from him but before the call ended she asked him if he had Mxit and that he should invite her if that's the case. Not long after that, they started dating. They would chat, call each other and talk on the phone for hours, almost every day, trying to make a long distance relationship work. They were dating for more than a month when Justin went to her house for the first time.

After that he would frequently make the trip to her house and they would come back to where he lived to spend the day together. After almost a year of on and off dating they broke it off. The distance had become unbearable for the both of them and they started to argue a lot. He was shattered, heartbroken; she had been the first girl he ever truly loved. He had made a promise to her that it was different and that this time he would abstain from sex until marriage but they were alone in a room so many times that he quickly let go of his resolve.

When the relationship ended, he battled to get over her and thought of her a lot. He remained single for about seven months after that. Until one day when he received an invite from a strange girl on Facebook and they started messaging each other. They would also send text messages and call each other. A few weeks after they started chatting, she was in town one Saturday afternoon, so they arranged to meet at the mall. When he got there she was waiting with a few of her friends who clearly wanted to meet him. He greeted them and then this girl (whom he only knew by virtue of Facebook and the calls and text messages they were exchanging), were off to his place. When Justin arrived home with her, they headed to his room; there was no one home. After talking for a while they started kissing and one thing lead to another and he sadly found himself back underneath the sheets. When they were done he could see it in her eyes, how disappointed she was that she had done the deed. He asked her if she was ok, her response was a "Yes" but her body language told another story. When the time came to leave, they made their way to the station, where she got on a taxi taking her back home. Later Justin called to find out if she had arrived home safely. However her phone was off.

Justin felt guilty and decided to end it right then and there, to just be friends, but the line had been crossed. Later that night she finally called him, an emotional wreck, asking why he had not called her. He then told her that they were not dating and he wasn't obligated to do that. They stopped talking to each other until two weeks later, when he received a startling sms from her saying that she had missed her periods. He immediately called her back to enquire about the matter. He had used a condom he remembered, so he told her not to worry. He ended the call telling her to keep him informed. Seven days later still nothing. He started worrying and decided to give her some money for a home pregnancy kit. He didn't have a job, Justin still lived with his mother and taking care of a baby was the last thing on his mind.

It was a Friday afternoon; he was at the gym working out, when he received the sms he had been waiting for. The message simply read, "I'M PREGNANT!!!!" Justin was in dismay;

his worst fears had been confirmed, he couldn't believe it. What was he going to do, his family, friends, everyone would be so disappointed in him. The girl was still in school and he was twenty two. He called her and they arranged to meet, and later they talked about what they were going to do. The agreement was settled, she would have an abortion and both of them would move on with their lives. The last he heard from her was an sms, which simply read "It's done!"

That baby could have been a doctor, lawyer, teacher, scientist, or even the next president of a nation. His careless actions and self-centeredness had hurt and betrayed the trust of so many.

"This can't go on!" Justin realized. He had lived this way for far too long, he was born again for almost a year but his actions did not match up to the convictions or creed he had committed to and believed in. So he decided to take it to God, and allow Him to replace his messed up view of relationships with His righteous standards…

Justin has been single now for little over a year and made the decision to stop dating, period. Owing to his experiences with premature relationships with the opposite sex, he has decided to put a hold on dating and use his singlehood to pursue his dreams and achieve his goals. As he has learned that sin carries within it the seed of its own destruction, so too he has learned that dating is a very destructive practice, as he has seen the results and the ramifications of his selfish, careless actions.

AIMLESS DATING

Like Justin, how many abortions have you maybe been responsible for? Or pregnancies, making you responsible for a child that you don't even want to take care of now? We date in haste, have sex, and we fail to own up to the consequences of our actions, and abortion seems like the easy way out, for we don't want to be exposed. The shame and stigma attached and associated with having a child out of wedlock seems too much to bear. Many people are just like Justin, they are out to have a good time, they don't know who they are, and in the process they violate and ruin their lives and also the lives of others. As a result we have teenage pregnancy at an all-time high; we have the mothers then having to raise the child on their own, or going for an abortion.

Women are also not the innocent victims in the things they allow to happen to them. She could have said "stop!""This is not me!"

Dear daughter, ask yourself who are you? Who are you that you allow yourself to be mistreated, used, violated and abused? Who are you that you parade, and show off nude and provocative images of yourself for attention and acceptance? Who are you that you would go to great lengths to sleep with a man and have a baby with him, in hopes that you may keep him? How many guys will you sleep with, when will it ever be enough? How many guys will have seen you naked? How many more families will you just be introduced to as the girlfriend? For too long you have acted like an innocent victim, afterwards you have been just as much to blame as the guy who you allowed in and who made you an accomplice.

Dear son, what is the measure of your manhood or masculinity? Surely you cannot determine that you are a man based on the parties, fast life and the amount of girls you can sleep with. How many hearts have you broken? Son, where are you, who are you?

Whether you choose to believe it or not, dating becomes destructive and is the drug of the masses that leave with it a bunch of messes. "I am just out to have a good time", "I am still young", along with a bunch of other excuses are what we say to rationalize and justify our perverted practices, while this cycle of dysfunction continues. It's in the songs we listen to, the movies we watch, desensitizing our threshold for pain, and making it okay to date without deepening in a sense of commitment, while the girl plays house wife, the guy is not even prepared to marry her. Even if they finally get married, the marriages vows taken become more and more meaningless.

Ask yourself, however, how long will you just be out to have a good time? How long will you aimlessly date, for the pleasures, when will you learn to treasure who you are, so that others will too? No matter if you were the victim, perpetrator or accomplice, you can start today to make a change by the choice you make. Your best you is waiting for you.

> **You see, your trials and failures in romantic relationships ought to have made you better and not bitter, there ought to be some gain after the pain you have experienced, and a testimony should have been birthed out of your test. Because what we don't learn from, we will continually return to and get hurt by.**

Other problems occur in our lives is a result of a defect in character and how we see ourselves, and we go to strange places and great lengths to be acknowledged, accepted and our worth affirmed. **Embracing the true you and breaking the cycle of dysfunction will sometimes require separation from former places and people who only enforced who you are not.** Aimless dating is just a game played by people who are unsure of whom they are. So are you ready to let go? Are you ready to say hello to the real you that you were always meant to be?

DATE WITH PURPOSE

You see, God desires to have people married because He instituted marriage. Any relationship that does not have the intention of marriage at the end is not from the Lord because why are you in that relationship if you are not going to honour that person by making him or her your wife or your husband? Why are you committing to something that is temporary, that is flimsy and that is not built on the foundation of Christ? **Many times we think we are in love then we find out it is really not love it is lust, or infatuation or any other emotion that the devil uses to derail you from the purposes that God has.**

God loves it when there is husband and wife who love and cherish each other and He builds us up to that so that we don't date aimlessly but date purposely. If you are a child of God, being in a relationship the way the world is in a relationship is not what God wants for your life. We don't play around with emotions nor do we say I love you when we don't mean it and that's the creed we need to uphold, we are His ambassadors and our words should be salted. Our way of life should be above reproof, our intentions should be clear; there should be no confusion, no ambiguity.

There should be no deceit, we should really live a life that is holy and pleasing to our Lord, so that when He blesses us with a partner who shares the same values that we do, who shares the same love and passion for our Maker and our Lord then we know we can go hand in hand and be assured that the Lord's blessing rests on us. The Lord is then always involved in our affairs, so trusting Him when we enter into a relationship and really looking for the things that matches up with his word will be a sure sign or check list that you can follow before you enter into a relationship.

I believe God has destined each and every one of us to find our own Adams and Eves. He also says in His word that some are not meant to marry, but if that word is not meant for you then obviously there is a partner for you, that He has purposed and designed and that will match you perfectly. Will you allow God to shape, mould and show you who you really are so that you may date with purpose?

SAY HELLO TO THE REAL YOU

People's behaviour won't change if they perceive themselves the same. Truth about you is not what people think you are, but who God says you are.

Our identity is greatly influenced by whom and what we identify with and knowing what you are not leads to a true discovery of who you are. When Justin finally realised he had a problem, it caused him to have remorse and desire to change when he accepted the truth of his actions. We will never desire true change if we believe what we do is right.

Through the journey of life, we get hurt, abused, raped, betrayed, violated, rejected, we fail, we fall and we are frail. We mess up, we mess up big time; finding ourselves in situations that seem like a mammoth task to recover from. Some situations can be so traumatizing that they cause us to question who we are even more and also form insecurities about "Am I still worthy to be loved? Worthy to be respected, honoured by another?" We ask ourselves these questions and often go to great lengths just so that we may fit into a mould so as to be acceptable to ourselves and affirm our worth to others and to feel valuable. Sadly, many times in the desire to be accepted, we become everything to everyone else but ourselves. Or you may define who you are in relation to others, while they also maybe unsure of whom they are. However, no matter what has happened, even though some things result from our own careless and selfish actions, God still had a plan for Justin and God still has a plan for your life.

I find that we are often too image conscious while we should rather be identity conscious, because who you are is not determined by your abilities, credibility, success or status, but rather who God created and fashioned you to be. You are created with talents, gifts and vast potential to become more and do more, you have to harness them and live your life to the fullest. For as my pastor, Dr. Pastor Maxwell Holland, says, "The image you have on the inside of you will always lead you to a place where you will express itself. It doesn't matter what people call you, it matters what name you respond to. As a man thinks so is he."

Many of my past relationships, if not all, were a result of me not knowing who I am. Thus I expressed this type of uncertainty in the life I was living and allowed friends and society to define who I am; I was a player, a baller, abuser, liar and a real jerk. This defined me, my manhood; it was the measure of my masculinity. It placed false expectations on what it means to be the man. However, I realized all that couldn't be me; I mean if God had good plans for my life, to give me a future, hope, to prosper and not to harm me, surely He would expect me not to inflict harm on others? I used to be so selfish, and careless that I didn't care about the consequences my actions had on the lives of those who could fulfil my needs and wants. However, God is loving, holy and just. He loves with the kind of love that once you are engulfed and overwhelmed by it, you can't help but to start being an extension of that love.

God created us, so that we may emulate His righteous standard and precepts as His sons and daughters. Therefore, you are not the liar, cheater, abuser, nor loser, but you are who God says you are. Righteous, pure, beautiful and lovely as His beloved, that is the real you.

Avoid going into a relationship not knowing who you are. Permit others to know who you are, people are not mind readers, our point of references are different. You therefore have to constantly teach people how to treat you. Try this, "I don't know what impression you have of me, but that's not me…" It's up to you to set the record straight! "This is who I am…", as soon as you make them aware of that, they will start honouring it out of respect for your stance and unwavering attitude not to compromise. Now say goodbye to the old you, and start embracing the new you, say hello to the real you.

Don't wait for someone to come dashing in and to be your knight in shining armour, or your superman. As good as that sounds, find your security and independence in God. Climb up to the mount, called, "All-You-Can-Be." Have fun enjoying you. I am mindful that even singleness can become a stigma, but cultivate a new culture that embraces singleness to the fullest and causes people to have more confidence in being single instead of being bored and intimidated by this season. **For, singleness is not idleness or loneliness but another season of purpose, a different shade that is part of the rainbow colours that explains the beauty and brightness of your life.** Take yourself out on a date, go out for movies with friends, explore. Don't allow anyone to rob the excitement and joy of this season. You don't start living or become alive when you are in a romantic relationship, start living today!

RYAN

BECAUSE HE IS SINGLE...

For a long time Ryan remained single as he was truly intimidated by the idea of getting physically intimate with a woman, feeling inadequate. This attitude was influenced by a habit of watching pornography which set false and unattainable standards of 'being the man' sexually in any relationship. This was a practice which lasted about 8 years, until the Lord finally set him free when he gave his life to Him for the first time. This decision was also influenced by the fact that as a teenager, he was overweight, and became insecure regarding his appearance.

He finally decided to engage in a relationship in his first year at the University Of Western Cape. However, this did not last long as his girlfriend was only interested in having sex with him, which frightened him. Whenever he thinks of those years of his life he really thanks God for having made him a 'coward', as it spared him much heartache, and getting sexually involved with that girl could have kept him forever away from Jesus, as such relationships have so often done.

Ryan wrote me a letter, giving his testimony of why he is single. He further explained how that in his early days as a Christian (which he realised more and more was only nominal – i.e. he was a Christian by name but not at heart), he was often flirting with girls, but he still had an inner anxiety about engaging in any intimacy. As a 'front' to protect himself, he decided to say that 'he wasn't ready', hoping that girls would just leave him alone, yet still allow him to flirt with them… This sounds strange, he knew, but the Bible isn't kidding when it says that, "*a double-minded man is unstable in all his ways…*"

He came to understand that the double-minded man refers to he who believes in Jesus, is charmed by His great love, and yet still holds on to his cherished sins and does not fully surrender, thereby allowing the devil foothold, and causes a to-and-fro battle in the man's mind, whereby while he knows what he should be doing is good, he finds himself only doing evil.

When Ryan eventually 'fell on the Rock and was broken', he came to realise that before he could engage in any intimacy, he needed to get intimate with his Maker. Before he could open himself up to a woman, he needed to open himself up to the leading of the Holy Spirit. Before he could know someone on a deeper level, he had to know who he was first as an individual on a deeper level and before he could find the perfect person, he needed to become that perfect person. He came to realise that when he is in his path of study, God expects him to devote himself to his studies, and allow Him to work in his life to will and to do according to His good pleasure.

He also came to the realization that he need not go searching for his 'loved one', for as God was with Isaac, so He would be with him, for God changes not. In other words, he believed that he can trust God with finding him a partner and making it evident to him just as He did with Isaac. **Ryan believed that we often downplay the degree to which God is willing to directly answer our prayers, in the same ways as He did with the patriarchs. Doing this and committing himself takes a lot of trust, but God wants us, just as He wanted Ryan to trust Him at all times, and to cast all our cares upon Him, for He cares for us. The mistake that we often make is we, especially as men, like to 'go hunting', and become like the disobedient Esau, who sought after women who knew not God.**

We dress smartly; act differently, all to find a woman. Where is Jesus in all this however? Does my searching involve Him? Do we search harder for a soul mate than we do for the Saviour of our soul? When we go hunting, and 'catch something', we sometimes become proud of our 'achievements', and our girlfriends become like our idols; soon we start thinking about them more than we do about Jesus, which, as sweet as it may sound, is a violation of the Law of life and love – God's law. He said clearly to us from Mount Sinai that we should have no other gods before Him, and this is as true today as it was back then.

> Ryan believes that the only time when he will be ready for a relationship is when he can think about his Saviour more than he does his spouse, dream about His perfection more than her beauty, when He is his first thought every morning, when He becomes first, last and best in every part of his life. Until such a time, he considers himself not ready.

Some might say, "Well, that will take forever!" If that's the case, then so be it, but he is not in a rush. Jesus has intervened in his life in miraculous ways, and he doesn't believe that He's about to stop. He believes that if he constantly strives to reflect His beautiful character, then he will draw only true and godly women to him, women who see Christ in him, and whose hearts will be sensitised to His love, and when that time shall come, as is consistent with His great faithfulness, God will make the matter clear to him.

THE ADVANTAGES OF HIS DECISION

The advantages of Ryan's decision, are that it is a chance for him to get to know himself better and for a deeper walk with God, thereby preparing him, should it be His will, for a Christ-centred, prayer-based, godly relationship.

Another advantage is that it gives him time to discover what God would have him look for in a woman. Too many are hasty in their decisions regarding marriage, which should be the ultimate goal in any relationship. **He does not buy in to the philosophy of 'testing the waters', he believes in prayer and fasting, and seeking God's counsel, he will date with purpose. There's no such thing as a blind date with God, for He will make it clear as the light of day if you only give Him time, and people often engage in relationships with those who might cost them their place in heaven.**

We don't realise the seriousness and solemnity of engaging in a relationship, as that person's relationship will ultimately impact your life, which is why you should ask yourself, what type of influence do you want? Will the person you desire to have a relationship with make you love your Saviour more, does that person just demand your attention? Does their spirituality dwarf your own? Will their companionship draw you closer or further away from heaven? Being single, therefore gives one time to discover these principles. **The most important criteria for a woman/man in my opinion are that they must never put each other before God. Christ is to be their all in all. Christ is to be the Solid Rock on which your love is to be founded, and prayer is to be the means by which you, together as companions, strengthen your grip on that Rock.** There are, of course, things like attraction and harmony of personalities, but these are secondary with regard to what I have discussed above.

People fail to realize, that whenever you are in a relationship, know that the person mirrors and is a reflection of who you are. When God presented Eve to Adam, Adams response was: *This is at last bone of my bones and flesh of my flesh…* (Genesis 2:23)**Now Eve was not presented to Adam until He had discovered who He was, stepped into His manhood and proved himself responsible.** You see Adam was first left to tend the Garden, he was given work. Work is attached to purpose. He was a steward of what God placed under his care. He was entrusted with a huge task, he was faithful and responsible. And you know what the reward is for being faithful and responsible?-**Credibility and more responsibility. If you are irresponsible with your own life you will certainly be irresponsible with someone**

else's life. So we justify our impatience and immaturity because we want to quickly get into a relationship. Being with someone, however, will sometimes greatly hinder you from discovering your purpose and who you are. Perhaps your purpose is to help others get into their purpose, but because you haven't yet discovered yours, you cannot help others step into theirs.

> We have too many irresponsible mama's boys, who just see our ladies as another mom to take care of them, while they play games all day, and are not driven by purpose, but rather their pleasures and own selfish needs and desires. We also have too many selfish, stubborn, dependent girls who don't want to make something of their lives and expect a man to come along and rescue them so that they can play the good old housewife. Ladies please, your purpose is not just to be a man's trophy or achievement; find your purpose.

Adam knew who He was, that is why He knew exactly what would fit him and be in unison for him. God recognized Adam's need for companionship before he did, and it is God who thus makes provision for that need, and as God provides, it is still up to Adam to decide. Like Ryan and Adam will you place that much trust and faith in God? Will you choose heaven's selection that God provides, or your flesh selection? We also have a choice; will we be patient and wait? For we are bombarded with a variety of mates to choose from, will we go ahead without God?

Also, Eve was a helpmate. She came to help meet the need because Adam was not only responsible, credible, faithful, eligible, but also productive. You do not need any help if you are not being productive. We draw what we are, one mess, plus another mess, creates an even bigger mess. You are either a mess waiting to happen or blessed to be a blessing, which one are you?

Because I'm single, I have a chance to not only learn and know who I am, but *whose* I am.

CHAPTER 3

PICKING
UP THE PIECES

DONA

I find it strange, that I am lost at this stage, and there are pieces of me, here, there and everywhere. Each guy I have given myself to, feeling as if each time I was busy losing a part of me, I need a change…

BECAUSE I'M SINGLE

"I am single by choice, well that is a statement that most single people like to make…" exclaims Dona.

At one stage of her life that is what she believed to be true. However, the truth is she was dumped or rather was cheated on and felt that she could not stay in a relationship like that any second longer, she had had enough! She was also afraid of becoming HIV positive and realized the relationship was a no-no and it had to go!

It was the Easter weekend she went home to Soweto to visit her family since she had been living in Cape Town for close to three years and had last been home a year ago. She had longed to see and be with her family. She finally arrived home and enjoyed and savoured her time there. Having visited family and friends, before her return to Cape Town, two days before her departure she had an argument with her mom, and in a fit of anger, she told her mom that she was going to become a drunkard, as she already had a bad reputation of some sort. Dona decided to just as well live up to it; not realizing that society, her past or people had no right to define her and determine the course her life takes.

She was truly lost at this stage of her life. Unknown to her, God already had other plans for her life. While being back in Cape Town, it was midyear when she moved from Gordon's Bay to Simon's Town which would become her new home and during this time almost all of her friends had boyfriends and she was the only one that was still single. By this time, God had also begun to deal with her and her alcoholism and she did the opposite of what she had promised her mom she was going to do. She didn't drink at all.

So while all her friends were busy, out and about partying with their boyfriends, she would stay behind and be bored with no TV, radio or any other form of entertainment. One night in August her friends came back from a night out clubbing, speaking about this one guy who was drinking and was just the worst drunkard they ever saw. **She didn't know what got into her but for some strange reason she wanted to date that guy so she could rescue him, she was lost, this guy seemed lost too, I don't know, but it seems true, if we attract what we are, then lost people will be drawn to each other too.**

She didn't even feel that she loved him, rather she lusted after him. Nevertheless she wanted to rescue him as she thought to herself that she could help him, unaware she needed some rescuing too…

A month later they started dating, and the relationship lasted only about a year. While in the relationship, she became born again, and then it started to be a dilemma of being in a sexual relationship and being born again. It slowly started to eat away inside her. She wanted to really pick up the broken pieces of her life and start over in order for her outside 'lostness' to conform to her inside 'found-ness' of her 'renewed-ness'. However, being in this relationship made it increasingly difficult for her as the days went by.

She wanted out of the relationship but didn't know how to get out, she would go to him to end the relationship but every time he would just sweet-talk her, and she would find herself underneath the sheets again. It was a vicious perverted cycle that began to torment her and drive her crazy inside, she was addicted, and their lust was the drug she was hooked on.

One day he told her that he had impregnated a girl. She was furious and so disappointed, nevertheless she thought to herself that this was her way out because she had been fasting and praying to get out of this relationship but didn't know how. As usual he came back to her, apologizing, but this time she pushed him away to go to the girl he had impregnated. He persisted, and sadly she quickly let go of her resolve again, accepted his apology and gave him another chance.

She could not understand why she was still with him, she felt that she didn't love him that much and even saw that there could be no possibility of a lifetime union between the two of them, yet she stayed with him. One night she decided to give him a surprise visit, it was Sunday evening. To her surprise, she found him with another girl in bed! She was devastated and stormed out of the room an emotional wreck! She then decided that was a good opportunity for her to set everything straight, she called him outside and with tears running down her cheeks, struggling to compose herself; she cleared her throat and said in a stern voice "you and I are over! If you ever visit it would be the worst day of your life!" She felt empowered, relieved and finally felt set free.

For a long time, whenever Dona had been single, she had viewed it as punishment but now she rather experienced how truly liberating it can be and realized that it is a process to maturity and for her to find herself; to pick up all the broken pieces of her life.

The relationship she had fell to pieces. When Dona decided to pick up the broken pieces, it was a result of her coming to terms with the sad reality of her plight; in fact she was fed-up with running around in circles with the same vicious cycle of perversion and dysfunction ruining her life.

However, after relationships that you hoped will work out have failed badly, where does one then go to from there? The truth of the matter is, things don't always go back to normal so soon, there is still hurt, pain and the sting of rejection. Not forgetting the guilt of the failure that one has to confront that lingers on. We are left fractured and heartbroken.

Whenever we experience a relationship failure on any level, whether it is a friendship or romantic relationship, it leaves us not only hurt, but broken. And every time when we get broken we become more disappointed, sceptical and hopeless, wondering whether we will ever be whole again, accepted and loved. Dona had a failed romantic relationship, in fact a string of failed ones.

SINGLE NOW...

We graduate with so many degrees, PhD's; we have even learned how to speak Hebrew and Greek, we are so called experts; we have gone to the moon and back. How can we be successful in so many areas and yet fail in making companionship work? It is because we have neglected to pick up the broken pieces of our life and when someone else is brought into the picture, instead of being the solution you hoped for, the problem is amplified instead.

Dona realized how many ladies are not dating yet are not single. She thinks that women have an amazing imagination. They can often say they are single yet are nevertheless in a relationship with a man in their minds without even realising it. Dona use to feel like one of them too often. She would make different male models her profile picture, or when attracted to one, she would imagine undressing him and think about all the stuff she would do with him... You see, being single is not about just abstaining from dating, but it's a time where one has to be single in mind, heart, body, soul and spirit; and still feel whole.

Dona is single now and yes, it may be a victory, but the fight still continues, and for the battle to be won in her life and especially pertaining to romantic relationships, she has to commit herself to uproot 'stinking thinking' and bad habits that have kept her there for so long, and which could take her back within an instant.

> She can easily revert back to old habits and practices, therefore committing to uprooting 'stinking thinking', is not just an option, it's necessary to conquer in this area of her life. Her singleness should be purposeful singleness and not aimless singleness. It should have an end goal in mind. There should be someone you are striving to become in your singleness who has not existed previously. It should be your desire not to come out bitter, but stronger, wiser and better as a result of what you have gone through.

A very familiar story comes to mind. It is the Biblical account of the Samaritan Woman who met Jesus at Jacob's Well. Jesus began to talk to her and then asked her to go call her husband. She responded by telling him that she had no husband. He then told her that she was right, that she had five husbands and the one that she was living with at the time was not even her husband…

Now if romantic relationships were measured by its success rate and ability to stand, surely she would not be the ideal candidate to choose and learn these principals from... I mean, it was as if she had mastered the formula of how to make relationships fail. If anyone needed to pick up the broken pieces, this woman surely needed to. Besides this, she must have been classified according to her actions. But here Jesus offers her a solution, a remedy; He says to her, that she is right. But it's not just that she is right and knows it, but almost like, "get rid of it, deal with it, how long will you carry on, and live like that daughter?" You need to locate yourself and pick up the broken pieces of your life.

> The reason we never get what we want in a man or woman is because we ourselves are lost and have never become that man and woman we were meant to be. You need to be what you want your partner to be. You cannot rescue them like Dona intended to, much less make someone into something they are not.

Also, you cannot engage the problem on the same of level of thinking that created it; to solve it requires a higher level of thinking. Unless you deal with the mind-set that created the problem and is responsible for where you find yourself, you are doomed to engage the problem the same way and end up with the same outcome.

Dona, although single now, is not free from the daily challenges she will have to contend with, so that she may triumph in her singleness before she finds companionship again, should it be the will of God for her life.

TAMING THE PASSION

In picking up the broken pieces, it's a struggle every day to stay true to a new chosen viewpoint because temptation is a constant threat. Taming the passion that is meant for a romantic relationship is therefore an ongoing battle.

> **Just because a womanizer, baller or player decides to change their selfish ways and assume another position, doesn't mean that it will just automatically happen, that it will be an overnight victory, or a walk in the park. In some rare cases it does happen that way but to triumph over these areas will require a continual fight.**

Temptation is vile, deceptive and deadly! It knows your name. Tailored specifically for you, it might not be the battle others are struggling or fighting, but it is yours. If you ever have been tempted then you know exactly what I am talking about. It interrupts; it disturbs and undermines clear thinking. It hinders you, brings you to a halt and it is what stops you from progressing to the next level. Mighty men and women have fallen as a result of giving into it, families have been destroyed and nations have crumbled all because they have given in to their lustful desires, as a result of being tempted and falling short of taming the passion.

Not all temptation we face is sexual temptation; we are tempted to lie, to steal, be proud, greedy, envious and jealous, to quit and even to kill! Being tempted is not the real problem; it's the giving into the temptation that results in problems.

I also get tempted, every time I see a couple, every time I see fun and excitement. Honestly sometimes it seems like nothing done alone is half as fun as when done with someone else. Also being one who in my sinful past failed dismally to tame my passion and as a result engaged in promiscuous relationships, the change has been the most difficult of battles. Whatever we are tempted by, be aware that we are the ones who have made provision for it. Either you thought you were immune, or you gave consent, or your guard was down. You may have been unaware and now you are left vulnerable, having to either withstand or give into those desires. No one can be tempted by that which does not appeal to them, so whenever you are tempted it is your prerogative whether you will entertain or evict it. Temptation suggests, appeals to the mind and once pondered on for too long, there is no telling where it can lead you. **You see, whatever enters the mind persistently, later forms a continual impression so hard to resist that you can't help but give into it, because even as you are you fighting it, you are focussing on it. Your life can change when you change your focus.**

In a perverted world we are bombarded with sensuality daily and because of that constant pressure it is an uphill battle trying to tame the passion and remain pure. That is why one has to be vigilant and cautious about the movies you watch, songs you listen to and conversations entertained, for it can and will easily be the trigger that causes you to be tempted beyond what you can withstand, derailing you off your set course. It plants seeds that will desensitize you to the point where you would eventually like to explore uncharted waters which could lead to your downfall and perils unknown.

No one is immune to temptation, and because of that there must be visible measures you have implemented to ensure that the integrity of your singleness, while you wait and patiently prepare for companionship, is not compromised. Know them, show them and uphold them. For the victory that we achieve in any area is in direct proportion to the measures we are willing to take.

I cannot remember how many times I have come very close to hook-ups, dates, and tight spots as a result of not being vigilant and cautious in how close I allowed the opposite sex to become without making my intentions clear. You could say I was okay with flirting with temptation, but not always prepared to face up to the consequences of where it would lead me.

Being clear in advance saves you a lot of unnecessary headache and heartache later. It will prevent having to apologize for not communicating your intentions right from the very start, and could avoid your kindness being misinterpreted, costing you a good friendship in the process. As a result of not being clear and upfront, there are a couple of friendships I know that ended on a sour note, because I was not prepared for all that the person wanted from me, and I had to repent, which could have been avoided. I was supposed to defend the lady, and stand guard over her. Yet, I could not see that we were enticing each other, giving birth to premature and unhealthy desires. Instead of taming the passion, we played with it.

> There is nothing wrong when people are drawn to each other, and gravitate more and more closely to each other, but when you are not ready to enter into companionship, it is better to be clear, rather than give false hope and leave the other person hanging.

Like the Biblical account of Joseph who decided to flee when he was seduced and tempted by his master's wife. **You see he didn't wait, or debate to see how strong he was, he decided not to entertain it, but rather escape and flee temptation. We too then realize the lesson that we were never meant to flirt with temptation but flee from it!**

HERE ARE SOME MEASURES YOU CAN FOLLOW, THAT MAY HELP TO TAME THE PASSION

Make Boundaries Clear, Make Boundaries Known

- Don't put yourself in unnecessary situations that become the breeding ground for compromise and disappointment and may leave you vulnerable to test the level of your endurance.

- Take responsibility for your purity: when we remain pure the way God wants us to be, it is marvellous.

- Resist the urge to classify what you are vulnerable to in reference to others; know your prohibition and limitations. If you cannot get to close to the opposite sex without resisting the temptation to continually want to get involved with each person you come across, then it is best to rather stay away until this area has been dealt with in your life.

- Avoid going to places and people that cause you to be in situations that make you feel uncomfortable and vulnerable.

- Restrict yourself from certain activities, knowing that if you cross that border there is a danger you may fall and turning back will be even more difficult.

- If you are friends with the opposite sex, avoid being all touchy and lovey-dovey if you believe it's placing you at greater risk to be tempted. If perhaps you need to tell the other person to stop, do it, but be sensitive of how you communicate it to them, because having the liberty to be that close to someone may be something foreign to them. Your approach must be one of love.

- Avoid going out late at night with the opposite sex, or hanging out together late at night alone. Rather have people with you who act as chaperones, guarding both of you from each other.

- Be firm about what behaviour is acceptable to you. Unless they recognize and discern your value, people will start treating you like trash, when you and I know you are a person of class.

GET HELP, A STRONG SUPPORT SYSTEM OF SAFETY

Sometimes we need help with picking up the pieces, and dealing with temptations, lust as well as other feelings, insecurities and perverted practices. Don't be afraid to ask for help. Those who care for us and love us are sometimes chaperones and wise counsel when we are at our most vulnerable and cannot think and see clearly.

I like what Dr. Ravi Zacharias said in one of the segments of his series, I was listening to, *I Isaac, Take Thee, Rebekah*, "When we get our hearts involved so quickly that our minds are not functioning anymore, we then end up seeing our parents as interrupters of a relationship rather as the wise ones assisting us to seek the right one."

Do you have someone that you are accountable to? Someone who keeps you in check and is not afraid to give you a firm rebuke out of love because they only have your best interest at heart? For those who truly care for us will sometimes tell us things we don't want to hear because of their overview of the situation. *Faithful are the wounds of a friend, but the kisses of the enemy are deceitful* (Proverbs 27:6 NKJV)

Those who care and look out for us are almost like guardian angels God has put along our way. To care, to love us, guide and help mould and form us into what God wants us to be.

COMING OUT OF BROKENNESS

Dona became born again, had been free at last from this last relationship. One could say she was now rescued, repaired, restored and set free, yet wrestling with maintaining that truth. **In our brokenness we are never what we should be, or were born to be but the end result can still be made beautiful again.**

After experiencing the trauma and drama of so many failed relationships you need to sit down and literally call yourself to some kind of timeout to evaluate where you are and pick up the broken pieces of your life.

Perhaps you have had a divorce, have lost someone due to calamity, been in and out of relationships, or been hurt to the point that you don't even see the chance of getting into a relationship again because of the fear that the cycle of dysfunction and perversion will be repeated. The fact is we do get hurt and are broken at times; so broken that giving up seems more preferable. **However I would also like to assure you that bruised, broken and abused things can become useful and beautiful in the hands of God.**

Dona tried desperately to make the relationship work, but they were not pulling together, but rather drifting apart because of their two opposing world views. There is also nothing wrong in trying to make a relationship work, but eventually if the trying is one-sided then you need to re-evaluate things. If the other person is not willing to fight for you, when you have been fighting for so long, eventually you will give up the fight too, just like Dona did.

Many times under closer examination you will find out that the desire of someone who continuously wants to be in a romantic relationship or *serial dating*[2] is not the real problem, rather an extension of the real problem and a cry out for help.

Relationships fail because individual's lives are failing and falling apart. They are in a mess, they are broken and having failed to confront the real problem, they create ten more

[2] *Definition of Serial-Dating: Dating continually, jumping from one relationship to the next, without even giving yourself time to breath*

problems on top of that. We can either step up to help them, or sit back and judge, criticize and condemn them. **If people don't learn to overcome problems in their life, they will tend to use a romantic relationship as a crutch to help them walk, instead of enjoying the time to complement each other and flourish together.**

Assess your real situation, when it has been dealt with, you may come to find out romantic relationships become workable and doable. **You cannot get married to the future possibilities of what you can be and have, while you constantly allow the past to invade your present.** Divorce it, deal with it, and pick up the shattered, broken pieces of your life.

In life there are a number of reasons and factors that leave us shattered and broken. I will highlight three common areas that I believe affect us in our romantic relationships

GENERATIONAL CURSES

Where you are born, your family and your surroundings become your point of reference that defines and impacts your life. They form your beliefs, your philosophies, the values you hold distant and near, what you value and what you disregard, your normality and abnormalities; it becomes your very first familiar picture.

The world is full of brokenness. Hurting, wounded, broken people are everywhere. Sometimes even our homes, the very first picture we view, may be distorted, a broken picture.

Because we portray and live out many times what we see, if sleeping around, and dating one person to the next is prevalent in the society you were born into, it is almost certain that you will grow up idolizing and gravitating towards it. **As a result we equate romantic relationships with violence, insatiable lusts, absence, adultery etc. If you were born into a home where dysfunctional, distorted and broken relationships were dominant, that maybe the type of life you will replay, for we mimic whatever mentors us continually.**

I grew up without my father, and I was born out of wedlock; my father was also born out of wedlock. Many people can trace the same behaviour that they may be practicing deeply embedded in their lineage too. My own father had many kids by different woman, so I have some brothers and sisters out there whom I don't even know. Without me even realizing it, or being aware of it, I too was heading down the very same path, as I was a player, a baller and a womanizer just like my father, you could say. **I portrayed and was proceeding to relive my father's failure to a degree. I was slowly on the path of perfecting my biological father's perverted**

practices. You see what we fail to defeat, we are likely to duplicate and repeat!

I never learned things like patience or how to practice things like chastity and purity from my father or how to stay faithful and true to only one woman. I could either conform to a generational curse that seemed prevalent and deeply embedded in my genealogy, or I could break it and make sure a new legacy is started and birthed out of my life and pick up the broken pieces pertaining to this area of my life. It is only by God's grace that I quickly came to realize where my selfish actions would lead me, and I promised myself that that kind of person is not what my future partner and kids deserve. That therefore became my new resolve and I was going to make sure I saw it through to become everything to my kids I wish I had had in a dad, and the great husband to my wife to be, that my mom never got a chance to experience.

Many other people are stuck, stuck in bondage, perverted practices and generational curses they are born into. Now instead of breaking it, and redefining what their family is known for, they just relive it and the cycle goes on…

Take stock of where you are, what are the good values that are strongly embedded in your lineage, your family that has been passed down to you? Take all and make use of whatever is pure, good and lovely, while you discard what is not. The generational curse doesn't have to go on, bury it, it ends with you!

ABANDONMENT

There is a psychological term called *"Deprivation dwarfism." It is a physiological concept used to describe children who have been physically dwarfed, because they were not nurtured, touched or handled. The lack of love and physical closeness literally caused their physical handicap.*[3]

Many sons and daughters are dwarfed in certain areas of their lives; they are dwarfed spiritually, physical, emotionally and mentally. They are dwarfed in boyhood, and girlhood. I call it boy and girl-phobia; watch out for it, it's a disease. It is a case of them having been abandoned, abused or deprived of the love and attention that would dignify their opinion, affirm their worth and promote their growth to assume their roles and responsibilities as the man and woman they were born to be.

They have thus grown from adolescence into adulthood dwarfed and handicapped. Although they can play

[3] Jakes, T.D. *Loose That Man & Let Him Go!* United States of America: Bethany House Publisher (Pg. 5)

with the toys of a man and woman they have dismally failed to become that man and woman because they have not assumed responsibility for their manhood and womanhood.

Some of our ladies have been abandoned and have not grown up with a father and a male role model who can set the standard for what becomes acceptable and what doesn't when other men come and show any sign of interest. Thus many times it has led them to misunderstanding manhood. In their search for that masculine touch and voice, they have gone out man hunting and have fallen prey for a man that can rock their world temporarily instead of a man of the word, a man of God who will be their rock. If he can love her and hug her, he can have her but a real man is a brother who will protect her and be a builder. He will not be slick or sweet talk her just to get into her pants. No, a real man is into real talk, not only that, but he walks his talk. Our daughters however, often fall for the counterfeit, because they measure a man by what the media, the world portrays, instead of what the Word teaches.

We have a lot of boys but few men, a lot of girls but few women. Becoming that man/woman happens by a choice birthed out of a deep-seated conviction based on who you are called to be at that particular moment, at that point in time, where it all changes, when the man/woman has to emerge out of the child in you, to forever step out, and step up!

Becoming that man does not happen at a certain age, but rather a certain stage. It does not happen by church ordination, circumcision, religious or cultural ceremony that signifies your entry into adulthood. Becoming that man/woman does not happen by an outward observation but rather by an inward consecration. *When I was a child, I spoke as a child; I understood as a child, I thought as a child: but when I became a man, I put away childish things.* (1 Cor13v11 NKJV) Companionship is not child's play; what is good for a man and woman could be dangerous for a child, or childish thinking, that's why it is imperative for man/woman to put away childish things.

I like what Bishop T.D Jakes says in his book, *Loose That Man & Let Him Go! "We court disaster when we carry childish perceptions into adult relationships."*[4] Children lack the spiritual, emotional, and psychological underpinnings of adults. As children they live life on impulse and reaction; as adults, you are to weigh and allow time to search, reason and verify facts from opinions and myths before you can come to a sound conclusion.

[4] Jakes, T.D. 1995. *Loose That Man & Let Him Go!* United States of America: Bethany House Publisher (Pg. 5.)

T.D Jakes further highlights, *"If as adults our understanding is still elementary and childish, we may come to immature conclusions. Childish wisdom can be the most dangerous of all- especially in the mind of a wounded adult"*[5]

The other day one guy told me his girlfriend was not treating him like a woman should. I said, "maybe it's because you not man enough either!" You are either a man or a boy, a girl or a woman. Which one are you?

1. The man is a man of note, the whole man. A man is a righteous brother, hard worker, provider, counsellor, honours his word. He walks with integrity, respects females and leaves an inheritance for his sons and daughters and future generations.

   A boy is selfish, blames others for his mistakes, is irresponsible, lives for the now, is experimental etc.

2. The woman is the woman of virtue. A woman that is mature in her thinking, groomed to perfection, independent, well-mannered, submissive, speaks when spoken to, walks with dignity and carries herself with grace.

[5] Jakes, T.D. 1995. Loose *That Man & Let Him Go!* United States of America: Bethany House Publisher (Pg. 4.)

A girl is naïve, impatient, dependent, self-seeking, and stubborn at times, the list goes on…

Abandonment often leaves one vulnerable and handicapped in certain areas of your life. Our sons and daughters who have been abandoned and left to fend for themselves are trembling in what would seem for them sometimes to be a cold, dark and lonely world.

If we don't have men and women willing to step up, fill the gap and teach them how to carry themselves, who will? They need to be taught to pick up the broken pieces of their lives, and in turn help others with the same advice, encouragement and wisdom that have worked for them, so they may become men of integrity, dignity, men of honour and high moral conviction, men of valour, men of God; with the compassion to uphold our women instead of robbing them of their innocence.

May our women find themselves in a position guarded and directed by God, one of submitting and service to Him; women of substance, significance, women of virtue, women of God.

THERE IS A MAN INSIDE OF EVERY BOY THAT IS WAITING TO ROAR, AND A WOMAN THAT WILL RESPOND TO THAT MASCULINE CALL!

ABUSE

One night as I was cleaning my room, I accidently hit over a glass and it broke. When I began to pick it up, I realized that I have to pick up the broken pieces carefully otherwise I will end up hurting or cutting myself. We are like that when we have been hurt, betrayed and broken. We carelessly go around and cut not only ourselves but bruise others in the process too.

You have perhaps allowed men/women to think for you; to put your own needs, agendas and goals to the side, while putting theirs first. They have not allowed you the time and space to heal and to address the root causes of behaviour and practices freely without disturbance or distractions. Now you are holding on to past hurts, disappointment and pain, feeling inferior, frustrated, depressed and bitter inside.

Perhaps your childhood was not too great either; you may have had abusive parents or no parents at all and moved from one foster home to the next. Worse, perhaps you were left homeless, wondering if God will ever take your pain away but no sign of relief seemed to come. Maybe you have even been molested by someone in your family, or by strangers. Perhaps you were told not to speak out, and hide those people's wrongs. When you have asked God to make the pain go away, and when it didn't leave, you became more angry and cynical and formed love-hate relationships.

That hurting, that pain, leaves us wounded and broken, fractured, shattered all over the place like broken pieces of glass; and one thing about broken pieces of glass, we need to handle it with care, we need to be sensitive with our wounds and allow them to heal, otherwise we could cut and also wound others because of our brokenness that never healed. Stop trying to make yourself or others compensate for the hurt, pain and abuse you have been through.

Picking up the broken pieces is a process of re-discovering and recovering your original identity, your purpose in Christ. Sometimes the purpose of the crushing and breaking is that we die to ourselves and our selfish ways. Unless we die to self, we will always try and just make a relationship work not realizing we need the strength and grace of our Almighty God to make a romantic relationship work and what it is, truly beautiful. **So many times we are crushed to make us aware we must begin to trust more and more in Christ, so that the picture may be perfected in Him.**

You are not a victim, but a survivor. You are still here, still alive, still kicking, still standing and nothing about where you were and what you have been through is as true as what God is about to do in your life, and what He has to say about you. Be still, He is still God above every hurt, pain, brokenness and whatever storm that seems to be life-threatening. Behold He is strengthening you; He is doing a new thing, restoring your dignity, brokenness and shame. He is busy picking up the broken pieces of your life, dear son and daughter; you have nothing to fear any longer, you are coming out of brokenness!

CHAPTER 4

EXHALING

> "EVERYONE SAYS FORGIVENESS IS A LOVELY IDEA, UNTIL THEY HAVE SOMETHING TO FORGIVE." C.S LEWIS

Are you over your ex or whoever hurt you? Does hatred, anger or animosity leap in your heart whenever you are close to them, hear or see them? Refuse to store up litter; you cannot start a new day, without letting go of the baggage and garbage of the previous day. Exhaling is all about new beginnings.

> There are so many healing benefits and rewards in forgiveness. Forgiveness is liberating. It cuts the cord between you and the past.

Forgiveness takes courage and it's a sign of strength. In essence, you are saying no matter how bad things were, how I felt, how I've been hurt, disappointed and betrayed, I am willing to let go, I am willing to move on and let it be, for it shall not get the best of me! Don't forgive hoping that the next person might ask forgiveness but forgive because it's what God requires us to do. Forgiveness is at the heart of

God, as the forgiving Father. God touched and moved our hearts when He forgave and loved us first, and He keeps on forgiving us. Surely, we ought to do the same as His sons and daughters.

There is nothing that robs our joy, and fosters strife, hatred, jealousy and envy more than walking around with unforgiveness. Unforgiveness keeps us tied to the past, unable to take a full, firm grasp of the present moment.

We may feel a temporary, superficial happiness and joy based on circumstances, and assume that something good must be happening in order to be happy and joyful. Joy is not joy that seems to disappear as soon as you are in a room with, or close to the person you have not forgiven or whenever you hear them succeed. Instead, let your life be a living testimony and a reflection of God's forgiving grace and unending mercies, ministering to that person, instead of mistreating that person through unforgiveness.

You have perhaps allowed unforgiveness to be like a wall in your path, making you unable to progress freely without the unnecessary baggage of the past invading your now. It has become a wound that could have healed a long time ago but instead has turned septic because it feeds off the unforgiveness you are harbouring. So you are shouting and screaming as if you're victorious but deep inside, something is lurking, eating you up like a cancer. Unforgiveness affects your life because you are trying to define and live your life based on what happened in the past.

You remain stationary; stagnant in some areas of your life because of unforgiveness and you are wondering why you not progressing; but the problem is that you are tied down to your past, and you've been held down by the weight of the burdens ever since they arose.

THE FIGHT OF FORGIVING

Some events cause us to experience what is commonly referred to as Emotional/Psychological Trauma. *Psychological trauma is a type of damage to the psyche that occurs as a result of a severely distressing event. A traumatic event involves a single experience, or an enduring or repeating event, that completely overwhelms the individual's ability to cope or integrate the ideas and emotions involved with that experience.*[6]

These are any extreme or shocking events that can be characterised as emotional and traumatic at the same time. These are unexpected and unforeseen events that can

[6] http://en.m.wikipedia.org/wiki/Psychological_trauma

render us basically powerless. They shake our world within an instant and forever shape our view of others and how we perceive ourselves. Trauma is caused by a number of events, for example, a car crash, natural disasters, being robbed, the loss of a loved one, being raped or a failed romantic relationship. It leaves us an emotional wreck as we try to escape and seek safety from the terror of that moment, leaving a blow to our self-esteem, dignity and confidence. This often leads to a person fostering bad habits to escape or numb the feeling; habits such as drinking, partying excessively and overeating, changing boyfriends/ girlfriends constantly (as I mentioned in the previous chapter, serial-dating. Be aware we have a lot of them, as it has become fashionable.)

These sought after solutions that I mention above hardly change anything because they are a temporary solution to solve a long-term problem. Avoid playing guilt-driven games or blaming oneself and rehearsing that tragic event. You don't have to continue the habit of feeling sorry for yourself and calling other people so you can have a pity party with them.

It would have all changed if we learned to let go, it would have all changed if we knew when we said, "yes Lord" it was forever nailed to that old rugged cross. It would have all changed if we knew that day we really became brand new. It would have all changed if you knew this new person you have become had never existed, and the life you live now is a life you live in the spirit. It would have all changed if you really knew He took every unpleasant, painful and bitter memory and experience; but you still find yourself still holding on, in a fight with forgiving, too scared to let go… At the end of the day, you cannot change what has been done or said. You have got to stop living in the past, it won't solve anything and it just perpetuates the trauma of that moment.

You have to refuse to walk in unforgiveness, refuse to walk in envy and refuse to walk in jealousy even though others might do so. It is fine for them, but tell yourself it has become unacceptable to you. You are washed by the blood of the lamb, sanctified and set free! Loosed from depression, loosed from perversion and loosed from the shackles of bondage!

I know you might be saying," You don't know the extent of what they did or what happened?" **Well when we try to measure the degree to which we've been wronged, hurt, disappointed or betrayed, we will never be truly free -because we are focusing on the problem, instead of seeking resolutions and solutions.** Yes, God forgave us and that is enough reason for us to forgive others; however we are not required to trust that easily otherwise we will be foolish and gullible. Trust requires a track record that is built over a period of time and can be destroyed within an instance.

Just because you have decided to forgive someone, doesn't mean they have to occupy the same place or be that close in your life again. No, it has to be earned and proven. Just because you have forgiven someone doesn't mean you will forget everything that has happened. God forgives and forgets, yet we are feeble human beings and it is sometimes very hard to forget when we have forgiven. A rape victim may forgive his/her perpetrator but what has happened is deeply embedded in her/his memory no matter how hard they try to forget. There are just some incidents that leave one with lasting scars, and certain circumstances or scenarios can trigger a flash back of that tragic event.

Now, depending on the degree of the event, and our response to it (which varies from one person to the next), this emotional trauma can sometimes just pass within an instant and in some cases last for days, months, and even years. It engulfs one in a world where you feel frightened and alone, scared to trust easily or forgive again. **At the end of the day, no matter what scientists, psychologists or counsellors may say, no matter what their research, reports, experience, observations or conclusions may indicate, God has the last say. When their research, exhausted to the outer perimeters of tried and tested**

formulas, has failed you, God will favour you. God will be able to help you heal and forgive within an instance if you ask Him to and if you believe without a doubt that He is able. However, even if forgiveness happens in an instance, the healing remains a journey, a process.

Forgive others for what they have done; forgive yourself for what you have done. In order to go to the next level we have to learn to let go, and let God. The thorn is small but enough to cripple any giant. You cannot hold on to the baggage of failed romantic relationships. **It hampers your growth and the potential for which God is preparing you.** God wants you to let go of the old so that He can do a new thing.

T.D Jakes was quite correct when he stated, *"If there is anything worse than the rage, the frustration, and the other negative things that come out of us, it is the things that do not come out! Festering wounds are dangerous wounds. A rumbling volcano is a dangerous omen, a solemn warning of a coming eruption that could rain down destruction on everyone living in its shadow."* [7]

You have perhaps not dealt with the issues but have simply tucked them away. However, just because something is out of

[7] Jakes, T.D. 1995. *Loose That Man & Let Him Go!* United States of America: Bethany House Publisher (Pg. 5.)

sight, tucked away, does not mean that it automatically doesn't exist. In time it may show, given the right circumstances it will bring down the entire house and everything else in its shadow. Perhaps there is a family member you have not been talking to, a friend you have not forgiven, because they might have said or done something and disappointed you. **Maybe you have not forgiven an ex-girlfriend or boyfriend for the way they have hurt and disappointed you, maybe it is you that needs to apologize, and ask forgiveness; whatever it is, if it is an unforgiving wound, I assure you, it will refuse to heal and forever limit you.**

STOP DROWNING IN DISAPPOINTMENT!

Besides wounds inflicted, harsh words once spoken, and wrongs that have been done countless times, there is nothing that corrodes us like unforgiveness. Families stay apart instead of reconciling and rectifying their mistakes, due to unforgiveness. By not forgiving, we open the door wide enough for the enemy to come in and rule and govern us.

Life will disappoint and betray us when we least expect it to. Life can be vicious and deceptively cruel, yet at times the disappointments we experience in life are just a set up to set us on a path of true discovery and a date with destiny. There will be no relationship that doesn't have its fair share of hurts and disappointments or even conflicts. It all often just deepens the relationship and makes it stronger. I mean, I don't only want friends or to be in a romantic relationship with someone that is with me in my highs, but friends and a companion who will be there in my moments of deep discomfort, controversy and conflict.

That's why it is not about who came and went many a times but about those who stayed through the long haul at the times you strayed and lost your way. **So when your romantic relationship fails, it is okay to be hurt and disappointed, but just know that life is setting you up with a date with destiny. Even fairy tales have their own dramas and dilemmas in the beginning but the end is always beautiful.**

Don't become bitter, for if your love doesn't overcome disappointment and past hurts, you will die lonely, bitter, frustrated and depressed. Disappointment, in essence, is one aspect that just builds character and increases your drive to persevere. Disappointment and pain we can all relate to, those emotions will either cause us to push forward to better places where we find peace and relief or will eventually become our drug of choice and keep us stuck at one station.

What you do with your disappointment and pain will determine what you gain. Don't allow disappointment to change the virtues and qualities you desire to have,

don't become mean because of past failed relationships. Don't fear to get involved in a romantic relationship again - one day when you are good and ready you will be able to make a relationship succeed. Be hopeful, and stop drowning yourself in disappointment.

During this life we live, before the light is dimmed and before you are aged, ragged and old, decide now to store up beautiful memories to treasure like gold, instead of bitter ones that will haunt you. Don't allow the seeds of negativity to continue to blossom, take it all to the Lord in prayer before it's too late and you hit rock bottom. Forgive and let go; pleasant memories will insulate you like a blanket, keeping you warm in the cold. What are you harbouring, what are you storing in your treasure chest? Make sure you are storing the treasures of righteousness. **Don't think because you failed so many times that you cannot put yourself through such grief and pain again. Don't let disappointment master, dominate or be responsible for eliminating you. You don't have to drown in disappointment. Exhale, your next breath will be beautiful.**

PART OF FORGIVENESS IS MAKING RIGHT

Many times we forget the many lives we have hurt due to selfishness and self-centeredness. Recently I was so moved by God that I decided to contact and inbox some of my ex-girlfriends to ask forgiveness and apologize for the jerk I have been. Below is my message to them:

Hey there how you doing? Long time since I have heard from you, I trust that you are well.

The reason I am writing to you is to extend my sincerest apology for the hurt I have caused you, lies I have told, the ways in which I have used and abused you. Forgive me for the jerk I have been to you in the past; for that I am truly sorry. I have experienced the grace and forgiveness of God to a greater degree and dimension imaginable and He is giving my life new meaning. I pray that you may come to experience this too. Grace, love and peace be multiplied to you. May your road ahead be a great journey, may you rise high and your future be blessed.

Kind regards El-Roy

- In forgiving we admit our faults and offences.

- We discuss to reconcile and resolve issues rather than turn them into an argument.

- We humble ourselves and share equal responsibility for the way things have turned out.

- We are sensitive enough to understand that owing to the way we have hurt someone, they will not always be that eager to forgive us, and let us close or in again. So we allow them the time to heal, while we pray for them.

- We decide to move on and change our ways so that we don't become repeated offenders.

> Perhaps you too feel remorse, like I felt; start taking responsibility, renew your thinking, change your ways and make right now if it is bothering you.

CLOSURE AND CLARITY

In any relationship, whether you are entering, exiting, or thinking about exiting, you need closure and clarity. Unless you communicate so that both parties are clear about where they are in reference to the relationship, you will be stuck between here and there; which is really nowhere.

Communication is vital in any relationship. Communication is the lifeblood of any good relationship and without it the relationship will eventually dry up and die.

Our points of reference are different, so people often do something to wrong us without them even being fully aware of it. They cannot read your mind, and may make assumptions and jump to conclusions if you don't communicate with them and say, "Listen, this is what you did then and there and I don't like or agree with it because this is how it makes me feel..."

You would be surprised to find out if it comes as a shock to them and they were unaware, but because you communicated it to them they will respect and honour it!

I had this one friend, his name was Mike, he had just come out of a relationship, and it ended on a sour note. What had happened is, one day Mike and his girlfriend Jessica had had another one of their usual arguments and this time they both had had enough! Mike stormed out of Jessica's place and never went back or spoke to her after the day of their fall out. Days, weeks and months passed by, no message, or phone call, not even a word was exchanged between the two. He thought that this issue between them was probably resolved and that they both must have accepted the fact that it was over. However, in his heart and mind he was going through an inner battle that was slowly tearing him apart, even though it remained 'under the radar', as he always appeared as if everything was fine. He was a very funny guy and could always entertain us with jokes.

The pretence eventually became too much for him to bear and he could no longer keep it all bottled up inside, it had to come out! So late Tuesday evening Mike came to me to seek counsel. He poured out his heart, told me about the incident and how badly it was troubling him. Mike and Jessica had just walked away from the relationship without bringing closure to it. Due to them not being clear with each other, things were left unresolved. Because of the way things ended, not having closure and clarity, it left them both confused and unsure of where they really stood with each other.

> The strength of our relationships is only seen in the testing of the relationship, but you decide what the definition and status the relationship will take. Whether you should be in close proximity or whether that should be altered and the relationship ended, whatever it is, you need to have clarity and closure on the matter, to know where you both stand.

I then advised him that when he felt that the time was right and he was ready, he should reach out to her and apologize for the way things had ended and left unresolved. I urged him to see if they could forgive and resolve past issues as they both deserved to know where they stood with regard to each other, instead of just leaving each other hanging.

Mike also then asked my assistance in helping him write a letter to her, to seek resolution. I promised him I would help him in whatever way I can, because, you see, he was searching for closure and clarity. They both eventually decided to go their separate ways and both agreed it was the best course of action for them, obtaining closure and clarity at last.

CLARITY

You need clarity so that you know where you stand; you need clarity so that you can make up your mind whether you going to accept being lied to, cheated on, disrespected and unappreciated. You need clarity so that you can make up your mind. You need a made up mind in order to get up and move on!

It is a dangerous thing to be stuck in uncertainty; we start doing things that are out of character, handling and doing things we never should do in the first place. This leaves you in a place of stagnation; it brings your entire life to a halt, like a plane stuck on the runway never taking off. **We can avoid so much hurt and pain if we are clear about a matter before it spirals out of control. Stop letting other people define your destiny; your life's purpose is not tied to them, be clear!**

CLOSURE

> If we are to build strong romantic relationships we have to learn to say goodbye to an unpleasant past that's threatening to ruin our present happiness.

You have been going through so many relationships and the reason they keep failing is because you just fail to close some chapters of your life, chapters that are meant to stay in your past! Closure therefore becomes imperative so that you can close that chapter of the book and know that when it is done it is done; it's over, and although it may have ended badly or on a sour note, you can look forward to what's ahead. The best is yet to come.

You need closure so that when you see him/her, there's not something that still jumps up when you hear or see that person, who says, "I still love you like that…" You need closure so that you can stop resurrecting dead issues of the past. You need closure and clarity in order to let it go and let it be so that you can become all you were meant to be.

ROXANNE

Do you find yourself sometimes amazed at the level or irrelevance of your relationship status? Well that's an ongoing factor in Roxanne's life.

She was fourteen turning fifteen, in high school and busy with grade 8 and to her it felt so good. She was still young, tender and peacefully innocent, in a world full of possibilities.

To her, it felt as if her life had just started educationally, socially as well as emotionally. Taking into consideration the different lifestyles young teens lead, for the majority of them the next few years will be the time in which they discover who and what they are and also discover what they like and what they would like to become and where they would want to go in life.

It wasn't long after high school started that Roxanne found herself in her first relationship, which actually turned out to become a real steady relationship for three years. Until her insecurities arose which were fuelled by rumours she had heard. She had heard that her boyfriend, the first boy she truly trusted and loved, was actually cheating on her with his so-called best friend.

Roxanne exclaimed to me, "We girls, we tend to lose faith in ourselves and the trust we have in our partners! Remember, we just recently entered high school and all these things are strange to us. So yes I started cheating and believe you me I tried stopping but I just couldn't…"

She was now engulfed in a world of passion and lust that took her to highs she never thought she could reach only to have her plummeting down to extreme lows later. It felt like a game to Roxanne, an awesome rush to see how far her lies could actually carry her. On the other hand, she was so busy doing her own thing that she did not realise that her boyfriend was doing the same to her. Their relationship eventually ended but the pain was so intense that suicide became a constant thought and an option to escape the nightmare of her present reality.

She realized however, that she had started gaining a bad reputation for herself by trying to play the same game and get even with her boyfriend…

She also realized that being single means being content with yourself; how you can get to know the inner you, and get to feel what it feels like to give your life a chance to exist on its own.

In her life however, she recalls how she never gave herself enough time to breath, a time to exhale; she continued having relationships. **She was good at keeping long term relationships going, instead of long term purpose singleness and was unaware of how she was losing herself in the process.** Parties, drinks, sex and weed were constant factors that were prevalent in her high school life. After high school her spirit became calmer. However she still went on to her 2nd, 3rd and 4th relationship which was a mistake which she deeply regrets and vows never to repeat. Nevertheless, she knew she would turn the lessons she learned into a blessing.

For some reason, Roxanne used to lose interest in romantic relationships easily but remained attached to the people she found dearest and closest to her heart. She found herself in two relationships where she was physically and emotionally abused. By the age of 20 she had already gained a reputation for dating indiscriminately… with the shame and stigma attached to it.

Roxanne's first abusive relationship was awful; she just couldn't gather enough courage to get herself out of the union. **It was a whirlpool of destruction but she was desperate to be part of this man's life. That was until he almost killed her.** One night, he showed no hint of emotion except anger as she lay face down on the ground begging him to stop hitting and kicking her. It then became crystal clear to her that it was time to move on or else she would cause real pain to the people who actually did matter in her life. It was not easy but she did it and she was very proud of herself.

Finally she met someone else whom she thought was her true love. In this relationship she was now also a contributor in all the abuse which took place, because she had not forgiven her previous boyfriend for hurting her the way he had and therefore she remained bitter.

She was often not only a victim but also a culprit. She had now brought all the emotional baggage into this relationship which was the worst decision she could have made. This relationship started falling apart after the first year because she started cheating on him, disrespecting him and simply just getting out of control.

From her first relationship she lacked confidence and guidance. She was too young when she engaged in emotions too mature for her to handle. Thus, now at the age of 20, she has had to learn the hard way.

We all have baggage. Not everything gets solved or resolved on this side of your singleness, but it is best to do all you can before you get into a romantic relationship. Don't leave room for unresolved issues. Instead of exhaling, carving out a new path and blazing a new trail, Roxanne allowed unforgiveness to engulf her, turning her bitter. The result was resentment and retaliation. As it is commonly said, "if you can't beat them join them." She chose the latter.

You don't have to follow the same path of those who have betrayed, hurt, disappointed and maybe rejected you. Love them, leave them and pray for them. In general, don't treat people based on how they have treated you. Don't be like them, be the light despite them trying to make your world dull and dark. What we fail to confront, often follows us. Conflict makes us stronger and the pressure brings out the best in us. You don't have to crack now, the storm is only passing and you will come out stronger as a result of going through it.

Unforgiveness causes us to believe that what someone has done is so unforgivable that it's hard to turn around. Unforgiveness is like holding your breath, and if you do not exhale you will eventually suffocate. So would you please learn to take a deep breath and exhale? Exhale everything that has got a hold of you, exhale for those that disappointed you, hurt and betrayed you. Exhale when you have been rejected, mistreated, broken and wounded. Exhale even when it doesn't make sense sometimes, I assure you, you will feel so much better afterwards. Roxanne finally learned to let go, instead of holding on, she exhaled and is single now.

> **And because she is single, she can reaffirm her morals and values.**

Because she is single, she can gain wisdom from past experiences to ensure they are not repeated.

Because she is single, she can move on to a brighter day, with renewed strength and vigour as a result of having discovered who she is in God.

Because she is single, she has rediscovered her identity, purpose and knows her worth.

Because she is single, she is content to draw closer to God.

Because she is single, she will learn new things and concentrate on being a better person.

Because she is single, she is keeping the faith and living well because you enjoy life more when you have a clearer aura and inner spirit.

Because she is single, she has learned to forgive, she has exhaled and this is the new theme song of her life:

"I'M NOT FEARFUL OF BEING SINGLE"

I'm single, oh yes, my inner being is not desperate

I will not marry because my soul is desperate

But mainly I refuse to philander because many think I'm irresistible.

Being single might be a taboo

But knowing your worth will be of greater value to the inner you.

Why cheat?

Why lie?

Why pay a bodily price to he who cannot appreciate the sanctification of your body as a holy temple?

When all your trust is in God, you can be alone yet not feel lonely

If you cannot be happy and content being single, you will never be truly happy with another being as your confidante.

Being single is being content,

Learn a new skill

Find a new friend

Start a new career

Win your own race

Be true to yourself, don't commit when you not ready.

Write poetry

Love deeply

Walk barefoot, and let out the kinder within

Pursue all passions within

Don't lose faith in God

Don't grow old, just grow you

Be fearful not, of being single…

Roxanne has exhaled, have you?

CHAPTER 5

GETTING YOUR **PRIORITIES STRAIGHT!**

We choose to rather play now and work later, take now and pay later. We want everything without the patience, diligence, commitment and effort that is required to get there. As it is commonly said, "easy come easy go." Easy go, because you lack appreciation for what you have and therefore it will just slip through your fingers. The reason is, the process involved in acquiring what you possess was either undermined, bypassed or handed to you on a silver platter and given to you prematurely.

The number one reason why we get out of sync, out of step and out of place and fail so much in romantic relationships, is because we have not realized how to put first things first, and we get our priorities totally twisted in the end! **We neglect to realize that love is not boastful, proud, or selfish; rather, love is patient before it is anything else.**

We are so busy trying to accomplish great exploits and even start our own families prematurely that we forget to seek or consult God on the matter. We are too wise in our own sight that we forget to seek godly counsel, then when it all goes wrong, when it all comes crashing down we want to cry and shift the blame - "Why did this have to happen to me? What did I do to deserve this? Why God? "However, we didn't start off with Him from the onset. You see, whatever we hope to accomplish, we have to get our priorities straight.

> It's amazing how quickly time can pass us by; the saddest thing is to realize that life has passed you by while you stood still. The reason why many people are bored to death and have a problem with being single is also because of not managing their time. If you don't manage your time, it will manage you. When you don't manage your time well, be assured you will not be able to manage your life well; you then either stagnate or regress as your life is at a standstill.

In getting our priorities straight, we organize, we pray, we plan and prepare.

ADDRESSING LONG TERM AND SHORT TERM/IMMEDIATE NEEDS

Let us have a look at two concepts commonly referred to as a Long Term, Short Term or Immediate Needs. There is a vast difference between a Long Term Need and an Immediate

Need, the problem arises when we do not know which is which.

IMMEDIATE NEEDS

Immediate needs deal with the now, what is current and apparent. One could say that our long term needs or goals are greatly affected by whether or not we meet our immediate needs. It is also very important to realize that we would not have long term needs without fulfilling the immediate needs. Some of our immediate needs are constant and others change due to the season we are in. For example, when we are babies we need to be nurtured, pampered, loved, cared for etc. When we grow older and mature, it is not that our immediate needs change so much as it is that now most of the responsibility has shifted to us.

When we were in school, we would play and have fun, listen to fables and stories that would capture and stir our imagination on the playground. We were kids and enjoyed our youth but that's not the primary reason we were sent to school. However, it was so that we could be educated with the right tools to empower us for our future career paths and occupations. If we are anchored in the right soil, encouraged and motivated, it fuels our determination, strengthens our resolve and tenacity to make it even through tough, trying times.

It is difficult to raise a family while you are still in school, it is difficult to raise a family while you are still being raised yourself and in our pursuit of love and belonging, we drift to the wrong places in our endless search for comfort, security and meaning. It is very sad when a child attempts to do a man's job. We wonder then why so many children grow up being raised by single parents, in dysfunctional homes? It is all because a child stepped up too soon and tried to do a man's job. When we don't get our priorities straight, it has a ripple effect and we are not the only ones affected.

It is therefore imperative that we get our priorities straight, for not doing so could set us up for imminent danger. Our long term needs should never overshadow our immediate needs. The problem comes when we are too busy day-dreaming about long term needs and goals. Not that that is bad per se, but we also then tend to forget about the present, we forget to live in the moment, in the now. You see, it starts with short breaths and small steps; it is one day at a time that brings us that much closer to our goals. It is of paramount importance that we therefore understand seasons and times, so that we may discern what season we are in and respond with the corresponding appropriate action.

Anything out of season or just off season is almost certain to have some deficiency. You see, we are in such a rush that we don't allow the process to finish, and we short-circuit the results of what could have or would have been; such as a flower picked too soon or an inheritance gained too hastily. Or such as an athlete running a long marathon and coming close to winning but starting to slack because he sees that he is close and the prize within his grasp. However, he doesn't bother to look who's behind him. Just as he is about to cross the finish line first, he gets overtaken and finishes second.

Later, he is disappointed with himself and he thinks after the race: "If only I had endured and persevered a little while longer…" You see, no matter the weight of the burden we have to carry, the opposition and persecution we have to face, no matter how long it takes and how much we have to endure, when we are committed to getting our priorities straight, the reward can be so much more valuable. We need to have a spirit of die-hard determination that says, "Come hell or high water, I am seeing this through until the end result turns out how I envisioned it would be!"

LONG TERM NEEDS

Analysing these is similar to goal setting and showing prudence or thought for the future. They deal with the steps and measures we implement to cater for where we are heading and not where we are and since we are constantly changing and growing, we also have to redefine or sometimes alter our immediate needs to accommodate or complement those long term needs. Our long term needs deal with what life we would like to live, the legacy we want to leave and what we want to be remembered for. There are a number of things that make up our long term needs/goals and it differs from one person to the next. For example, I would like to get married one day and have a family and kids. So my long term needs/goal will be to empower, educate and deepen my relationship with Christ, in order to be a blessing, a provider and to be able to take care of the needs of my family. **Know that love is good but it does not have to be an excuse for ignorance, no, I should apply wisdom.**

A lot of people get married but they continue living with their parents, or perhaps don't even have a proper job. Their life is a mess and on top of that they get married in debt and create even more debt; slowly cooking up their own recipe for disaster.

They rush to get married and then bring children into the situation. They then realize that they can only send them to particular schools, eat out at particular restaurants, and go on holidays at particular places because of the limitations of their finances. Both parents also now have to work longer hours because they are in debt. They may also have a desire to study further in pursuit of higher positions which mean better salaries, in the hope that this may alleviate some of the burden. Longer hours at work to earn overtime pay, and even going to study at this late stage in their life, leads to them neglecting their children and husband and wife neglect each other too. Lack of quality time then causes friction and tension in the relationship. The resulting chaos and conflict could have been avoided if only they had been patient enough to plan properly and get their priorities straight. Instead **they find themselves in poor circumstances because they planned poorly and thus succumb to being the surviving family instead of the thriving one. Let me be frank with you, a house is built on more things than just, "we are in love!"**

Love will not pay the bills, put my kids through school or place food on the table. In order to be economically secure, mentally tough, emotionally stable and spiritually mature, to be the provider and protector as the head of the house, there is no greater time to start and prepare for them than this present moment. Not that this will necessarily guarantee a happy home; however, it will provide more time and options in life. I won't have to break my back and work hard and long hours, just so I can provide for my family, depriving me of the quality time I could have had with them.

In the movie *The Great Debaters,* Professor James Famer, sr. lived by a motto "Do what you have to do and then do what you want to do", something I believe his son later subscribed to; thereby getting their priorities straight!

However, we hardly ever think about these things. No, love has blinded us; it has disillusioned us and clouded our better judgment. Wait until the honeymoon phase has passed, and the bubble has burst and it's time to face reality! You see it is not wise to get married and then realize you have not prepared adequately to meet the demands your family makes on you; it's enough to have anyone guessing, stressing and frustrated!

> **Get a job, pray, plan and prepare for your family. Invest, save for retirement and get into tip top shape! Being single is a time of maturing, learning how to manage resources, talents and gifts wisely as you tap into and maximize your fullest potential. You will never be able to manage companionship well, unless you have mastered the art of managing your life well. I am getting my priorities straight, will you?**

Some individuals are rejected, dejected and have been discouraged because of the low blows life has handed them. Some will either conform to the way circumstances have conditioned them or blaze a new path, with the hopes of a brighter day. At the end of the day however, it doesn't matter which class you were placed in or which home you were brought up in, as long as you stay focused and keep your eyes fixed on it you can reach your goal; as long as you choose to get your priorities straight! You know who you are, and where you are going; come on, stay focused now!

Written by a COLLEGE GIRL before she

Gave up the ghost...

I Took Off My UNDERWEAR...

I used to be that innocent girl who had the world at her feet. I was beautiful and I had eyes and hips that could make men swoon, and to top it all, I was a Christian; a very good Christian with a heart burning for God.

When I entered the university, I met a guy, his name was Derrick. I couldn't believe my luck the first time I bumped into him on my way to class, he had such a kind smile and a tender look that weakened my knees when he spoke. .

As I was late for class we couldn't talk much but barely three weeks later, I met him at the fresher's night party and I was overwhelmed. We got talking and I found out that he was in his second year and from that night, we became an inseparable pair.

At first, we were friends and as months passed by, we got closer and closer; the chemistry between us was undeniable.

A year later, Derrick and I started dating. He was everything a girl could ever want, save the fact that he wasn't so much of a Christian. Derrick had magical hands that made him hard to resist and most times I fell for it. At first I felt bad but when I couldn't help falling into the same pit I killed the guilt inside. One day, one of my friends said I was getting fatter and that got me thinking and I began to link the dots…first I had been vomiting every morning which I thought was due to the flu and then I had this morning sickness which I felt was due to stress and then my missing period…oh no it can't be possible I said to myself, I couldn't be pregnant!

After a series of tests outside school, I realized the awful truth, I was indeed pregnant. I was only nineteen, I still had my whole life ahead of me, what was I going to do? I couldn't tell my parents, they wouldn't hear of it. I had to go to Derrick to tell him what I had found out.

On telling him, he flew into the worst temper I had ever seen in my life. He was hysterical, calling me all sorts of names and I started crying heart-wrenching tears of hurt and betrayal.

When he looked into my eyes he must have realized how scared and hurt I was and so he pulled me close and ran his hands through my hair until I had calmed down and then said to me in the most subtle voice ever, "why don't you have an abortion". I pulled back instantly, I couldn't have an abortion! However, when he talked about my parents and the sanctioning of the college and the fellowship which I belonged to, I knew I had no other choice.

Derrick made all the arrangements and so on the appointed day we went to the room-like clinic. I shivered all the way there but Derrick kept telling me that it would be okay and that he was proud that I had made such a brave decision. When I entered the room where the abortion was suppose to take place I lay down on the table trying to dissociate my mind from what I was about to do. A young man then told me sternly, "you know I can't perform this procedure with your underwear on" and only then I began to pull them off. As I did this a sense of guilt overwhelmed me, first I had pulled off my underwear for pleasure and now I was pulling them off to get rid of the stigma the pleasure had brought…I felt shameful and exposed.

Every time that I felt instruments going in and out of me I kept thinking of the woman I had become and the hypocrite I had transformed into. I let out a sigh, if only I can get through this I muttered… if only…and then I felt a sharp pain shoot through my whole body. I screamed but the doctor told me to be quiet.

I felt another pain but this time I bit my lip and the pain then began to come in waves. I instinctively knew that something was wrong but I was too weak to talk or to move and then I heard the voices of Derrick and the doctor talking about the fact that I was bleeding excessively. The pain was unbearable and I could feel myself getting weaker and weaker. With the last strength left in me, I pleaded with God, "Oh Lord I'm so sorry for taking my underwear off, please forgive me." I drifted into a world where the pain seemed less hurtful and the voices became more distant.

Friends, our bodies are the temple of the Lord… Do not take off your underwear when the time is not right. Lots of girls who gain admission into university as virgins eventually lose their virginity so cheaply to guys who have nothing to do with their destinies. In a bid to get a certificate, they sell out for a destiny that a certificate cannot guarantee.[8]

The pursuit of love doesn't have to lead to the betrayal of faith, and losing one's purity, one's virginity.

Sons and daughters, don't take of your underwear when the time is not right, whether you have found yourself in that place before or not, make sure today that it's the day

[8] http://www.naijapicks.com/2012/12/a-true-life-story-written-by-college.html

that you will set things right. By His grace and get your
priorities straight!

CHAPTER 6

PROCESS
ME FIRST

> If you have never experienced the joy or seen the value and beauty of being single you will go into a relationship having misunderstood the purpose of the season you were in. For, before God pairs you, He will take you through a process, where He prepares you.

Our lives undergo a series of events, a cycle of courses, knocks, turns etc. Thus we are conditioned through the many processes of life itself. We cannot expect to achieve a different result with the same input. Changing the input, changes the output. What you put in is what you get out.

To be processed entails understanding that there are things in our past that have formed layers of junk or baggage, which keep you tied to the past and in bondage. These are wrong ideas and beliefs that often shape how we view things in the world around us. They stem from our social interaction, upbringing, our cultural and educational background that have indoctrinated us with a candy-coated lie contrary to His word and leads us down a perverted path of destruction. **Many people want to get married, but why should the process leading to marriage be such a perverted practice, instead of something beautiful?**

Being single is not a dead-end station that is dull and mundane but rather, it is a season to invest a good part of your life into cultivating healthy habits, building soundness of character, discipline and other virtues that will make you more effective, bring enrichment and wholesomeness to your life as you move towards the one God chooses for you when you are good and ready for companionship.

Hence, God first takes you through His process, where He schools you; just as He took the Israelites through the wilderness. Although the wilderness period may be painful and frustrating at times, it's the time where He has to deal with your Egypt, to take Egypt out of you. The Egypt years are symbolic of wrong beliefs, misplaced values, pride, arrogance, unforgiveness, bitterness, along with everything else you might be harbouring that originates from those bondage years. That old perverted system has to be replaced with His purposes, so that you might graduate to the place of promise after the process is done.

To graduate and advance from one level to the next is a sign of maturity, of growth. You remain stagnant at some stations in your life; all because you want to bypass the process and not learn the lesson and pass whatever test it is that will prepare you for the next phase.

There are some things you will never be ready for unless you have grown and matured to be ushered into the next level, season or phase. As a child grows up, he goes from learning simple things to deeper things. He is taught to handle things firmer with his hands as he adapts and his mind learns to grasp more and he is able to comprehend the complexities of life; too much, too soon would be detrimental.

- Sometimes, in the midst of being processed after you have surrendered to Him, it can be frustrating to see others around you in blossoming relationships while you have so many failed ones. However, you are currently on another journey that has to be processed to get to your promise.

- I know you sometimes wish it would already be time but be patient, trying to short-circuit the process leaves one with poor results and His timing is perfect.

- You will be pressured by circumstance, but keep on pushing while you are being processed.

- Being single can get very boring and lonely, to the point where you wander off and sometimes do things that are unbecoming of the person you are striving to be. Whenever you have fallen or strayed in your commitment however, get up, recommit and try again.

PROCESS OF PURIFICATION

Remember the Biblical account of Esther, an orphan woman, who also had to first undergo a process, a journey of her own before she was considered worthy for the king. It was a process of purification and preparation. She was a beautiful young woman to start off with, but was she a queen?

Don't ever settle for less than the best. It's a tragedy how our ladies sometimes devalue themselves. They have a chance to become someone's princess yet they settle to be someone's mistress instead.

> Dear daughter, whoever told you fairy tales don't come true or exist, I guarantee you they haven't met their prince charming. If he doesn't treat you like a queen, he may be charming, but definitely no prince charming. For kings understand protocol. You're a queen. Not glass, but a diamond, not trash but treasure. So don't settle to be someone's

> mistress when you have the chance to be
> someone's Mrs. Know your worth, think like, talk
> like, walk like and act like a queen and your king
> will come to you!

Esther had to complete twelve months of preparation prescribed for women, a process that would define and determine whether or not she was ready, eligible and fit to assume the role, responsibility and perform the task of a queen; for being a queen is not about beauty but duty. If she were not prepared she would have failed dismally.

For men and women alike, this time is vital, it is not just a time for them to sit by idly waiting while life passes by, constantly searching for Mr. or Mrs. Right. This is a time for discovery of who they are in Christ; cultivating and maturing in the values and principles that pertain to becoming God's man and woman first before anything else, while they are being processed.

> Charo & Paul Washer have written a brilliant and
> insightful article about the story of Esther, from
> which I gleaned and learned so much. The title
> of the article is

BECOMING ESTHER

It places emphasis on the value of singleness. Below I have highlighted some of the points out of the article and applied it to both men and women, since I believe in its entirety it speaks to both genders:

1. *Esther had to be transformed from a young lady into a queen before she could wear the title and fulfil the role.*

    *   *Hence, single men and women should learn the way of the Kingdom of heaven before they are united with the one God is preparing them for. They must be prepared intellectually, emotionally and spiritually, not by court attendants in some pagan temple, but by God Himself, His Word, and by other godly women and men who have been prepared before them.*

2. *Be mindful that in your singleness season, that you are not the only one single and that it would be such a tragedy to finally meet up with your husband or wife to be, only to realise they had maximized and triumphed in the single years by discovering God's purpose for them, pursuing and serving Him passionately and preparing to be a better husband or wife; while you did neither.*

    *   *Delight to look and remember as a single, it is a time of*

seeking God, being faithful to Him and His purposes. Also, trust in His timing.[9]

They also further highlight the wisdom of debunking beliefs that are prevalent in our perverted society:

One of the greatest lies is that if you do not, "have someone" or are not "actively looking" there is something wrong with you; or they think that they should be dating around as if looking for a husband or wife was the same as shopping at the mall.

- *An even greater lie is that single men and women should be giving away their affection indiscriminately, so that they may be more, "experienced" and know what to finally do when they have found the man or woman of their choice; it's a lie and an affront to God to say experience is the best teacher, when in fact it is God who is the best teacher, and though the world's motto is, "live and learn," the Bible's advice is "learn and live".*

- *You don't need to be experienced; you only need to be knowledgeable of what God has said and to be obedient to it. You should not be looking for the husband or wife of*

[9] Washer, C. & Washer, P. *The Godly Woman, Becoming Esther*. An article first published in Heart Cry magazine Volume 3, January 1998. ©

your choice, but should be waiting on the man and woman of God's choice; so that when he or she comes, it will not be past experience that makes the marriage work, but past chastity, purity and godliness.[10]

> The regret of not having maximized the potential of what they could have become in single years for a man and woman now married can be agonizing. Marriage is ministry, and unless we are prepared for it spiritually, mentally, physically and emotionally we will mess it up big time!
>
> Therefore, if you really want to be prepared for your partner one day, understanding the need to be processed is vital.

The desire to be processed and purged only comes after a true discovery of who you are in Christ. For once you have discovered who you are in Him, you will understand what you lack, and what you need. After raw minerals have been extracted from the ground, the discovery of their worth and potential, leads to the desire to process them in order to harness what they offer, their true potential. Their value

[10] Washer, C. & Washer, P. *The Godly Woman, Becoming Esther.* An article first published in Heart Cry magazine Volume 3, January 1998. ©

is also raised after they have been processed, for, they are refined and polished. So the process God wants to take us on just like Esther, is so that we can come out pure, refined and polished.

> **It is also understandable to note that the product is a result of the process.**

I particularly like the life cycle of a butterfly - before it becomes the beautiful butterfly we all know, admire and love, there are four stages that it has to pass through. There is no shortcut or bypass through each of these stages, for each process has its significance and serves its own purpose. I would like to use it as an illustration.

The four stages of the butterfly are as follows: It starts out as an egg, then becomes a larva, then a pupa till eventually it goes through its final metamorphosis, its transition to the butterfly. Here in this chapter I will deal not with the 1st, 3rd or 4th but the 2nd stage, the larva (caterpillar) stage.

They are not in this stage for very long, but in this stage they eat a lot and instantly start growing, their skin doesn't stretch or grow, so they grow by "mottling" (shedding the outgrown skin) several times while growing.[11]

---

[11] http://www.TheButterFlySite.com

That is what should happen when we are processed, the shedding of the excess waste, toxins, and baggage that keep us from growing and progressing. What should happen in relational-mottling is the discarding of what doesn't work and taking in of the word, so that we learn from God what works.

To be processed means peeling off the old, and putting on the new; to learn in order to grow strong. It is when we become equipped and prepared.

Jane understood this process

JANE

BECAUSE I AM SINGLE

"I am single because for a very long time I consciously and subconsciously avoided any type of romantic involvement with the opposite sex." Jane explains.

There are multiple reasons which contributed to this avoidance. She was sexually abused during her childhood and this resulted in her associating shame with the type of intimacy God created for the marriage covenant. She somehow saw physical intimacy as something bad and shameful and avoided such encounters with men. Her relationship with her father was strained for the most part of her childhood and as a consequence she has been fearful, cynical and wary of men in general.

She grew up feeling different and somehow defective, as if there was something wrong with her and she became a high achiever at school in order to prove to the world that she was worthy of love and acceptance through her achievements. Jane thinks that her competitive spirit intimidated the boys at school because none of them really ever showed any interest in her. In her mind this confirmed the deep-seated belief that she was not worthy of love.

When she was in her final year of high school, she dated a guy who was 10 years older than her. She was very fearful of any physical intimacy and it took her five weeks after they had started dating to allow him to kiss her. She often thanks God that the guy was a God-fearing man and that he was gentle, patient and respectful towards her. She was never placed in a compromising position, but her attitude towards physical affection really hurt her boyfriend and left deep scars on his self-esteem and they eventually broke up.

During Jane's second year at university, the emotional pain just got too much for her. She had tried very hard to pretend that everything was ok, but deep inside she felt dead. She hit an emotional rock bottom. She had developed an eating disorder during high school and realised that she was destroying herself. She needed God to heal her but she was afraid of allowing Him too close. She had begun to confuse the characteristics of her earthly father with her heavenly Father.

Jane realized that she needed help and once she started reaching out for help God sent the right people across her path. He worked through them to lead her to Him and to start seeing Him in a different light so that He could start processing her and transforming her heart so that it conforms to His righteous standards. This is when she realised that she could not get involved in a romantic relationship until God had purged, processed and healed her hurting, weeping, wounded soul.

> Jane also begun to realize that one cannot approach a romantic relationship when you are broken, empty and hungry to be loved; because one will never be filled through the love of another human being. In order to have a healthy relationship where love can be given and received, you need to have love in your heart to give and you need to believe that you are worthy of love. If you don't believe you are worthy of love, you will always be rejecting the love that is shown to you and will keep feeling empty inside.

It has been 19 months since Jane started recovering from her eating disorder and God has worked an absolute miracle in her life and in her heart. He has been incredibly gentle, kind and compassionate, and therefore she knows that when the time is right God will introduce her to a man with a beautiful soul and a heart for God; someone He has chosen just for her. She believes and trusts He will do this because she has asked Him to write her love story. This is Jane's prayer:

I am praying about my future husband

Abba Father, I pray for a special man.

A God-fearing man with a beautiful soul;

Someone who is a spiritual leader, someone I can respect.

A man full of integrity, diligent, aspiring, honest and true to his convictions.

Someone that is not easily swayed from the right, a wise, hardworking man;

A tender-hearted, compassionate, gentle man who loves people, children and animals too.

A man who works well with money and is not self-obsessed.

Someone who will challenge me to grow and love to see me use my talents for You.

Someone who will not be intimidated by my strengths.

A man who admires beauty, intimacy and adventure.

A best friend.

A companion.

Someone I can pool my talents and skills with and with whom I can glorify Your Name.

Someone who will hold my hand and love me for me.

A man who will protect and cherish my individuality and with whom I can feel safe.

Please keep this special man safe until You have worked in my heart and made me into the woman You want me to be.

Process me so that I can be the type of woman this man needs.

Thank you I can entrust my heart to You.

That I can trust that if You are in charge of my love life, the end result will be beautiful and well worth the wait…

Thank you that You made us for love, but that You love us too much that You do not just want us to bestow our affections on anyone and receive just anyone's love.

Human love has been corrupted and that is why we need to submit our romantic relationships to You so that You can keep us safe. Thank you Jesus, Amen.

I know He will do this, because I am single I have asked Him to be the author of my love story.

Salvation is not just an event that happens once, but rather a process of recapturing and identifying with our original identity in Christ; a process of learning to live a new life, living not by one's own standards or the standard of the norms around you.

So in the process of Jane's singleness, she would wake up in the middle of night just to speak to her Father, her Lord and Saviour. In the process of singleness, prayer was her confidante and worship was her best friend. She learned to start and end her day in prayer and also throughout the day. In the Biblical book of Corinthians the Apostle Paul speaks about how the affairs of an unmarried person are the things of the LORD, and that scripture was proven in her life.

Entering the presence of God without feeling any guilt, Jane wishes that so many of our ladies and men would become single not just by choice but by purpose, to be purged and processed before companionship.

You can never expect someone else to fill the void in your heart. If you have been hurt by life's betrayals, go to Jesus, so that He can heal your heart and restore it. You must find your completeness in God before you link yourself with someone or it will never be a successful relationship. God is restoring Jane to wholeness and purging and processing her for her partner to be.

Her prayer shall be answered, and He can do the same for you…

So before you ask Him for the perfect partner, have you made it your prayer to ask Him to purge and process you first?

CHAPTER 7

DON'T CATCH ME OUT OF SEASON

Spring, summer, autumn and winter; there is a certain mysticism and beauty in the changing of the different seasons. However, the change of seasons doesn't happen all at once, it's a journey, a process. From one phase to the next, with a unique purpose, as the journey of a new born baby starts off crying, cuddled and nurtured in the bosom of the woman who bore him/her. The baby doesn't just leap, but crawls to get adapted and acquainted to his/her new environment, accompanied by falling and stumbling but eventually learning to stand, walk and run at a later stage.

Have you learned to stand? It's only once you have grown mature enough in one phase or one season that it's possible to stand, walk and run in the next; recognizing the necessity of the inevitable shift. The day the baby recognizes it's time to stand, is the day the baby has adapted well enough to his/her environment and has matured enough in one phase so that it's possible to stand, walk and run in the next. **I know why standing doesn't happen all that easily – it is because** you need strong legs to stand and for you to stand longer, your legs have to grow even stronger.

> I cannot be irresponsible with where I am currently at as a single person and expect to be responsible and succeed in a relationship. Being in a romantic relationship with someone, will greatly be shaped by whether or not I have learned to stand, as a single. So until then, don't catch me out of season...

A story comes to mind:

"STRUGGLE IS GOOD! I WANT TO FLY!" "I WANT TO BE IN A RELATIONSHIP," WE SAY!

Once a little boy was playing outdoors and found a fascinating caterpillar. He carefully picked it up and took it home to show his mother. He asked his mother if he could keep it, and she said he could if he would take good care of it.

The little boy got a large jar from his mother and put plants in it for the caterpillar to eat, and a stick to climb on, in the jar. Every day he watched the caterpillar and brought it new plants to eat.

One day the caterpillar climbed up the stick and started acting strangely. The boy worriedly called his mother who came and understood that the caterpillar was creating a cocoon. The mother explained to the boy how the caterpillar was going to go through a metamorphosis and later become a butterfly.

The little boy was thrilled to hear about the changes his caterpillar would go through. He watched every day, waiting for the butterfly to emerge. One day it happened, a small hole appeared in the cocoon and the butterfly started to struggle to come out.

At first the boy was excited, but soon he became concerned. The butterfly was struggling so hard to get out! It looked like it couldn't break free! It looked desperate! It looked like it was making no progress!

The boy was so concerned he decided to help. He ran to get scissors, and then walked back (because he had learned not to run with scissors). He snipped the cocoon to make the hole bigger and the butterfly quickly emerged!

As the butterfly came out the boy was surprised. It had a swollen body and small, shrivelled wings. He continued to watch the butterfly expecting that, at any moment, the wings would dry out, enlarge and expand to support the swollen body. He knew that in time the body would shrink and the butterfly's wings would expand.

But neither happened!

The butterfly spent the rest of its life crawling around with a swollen body and shrivelled wings.

It was never able to fly…

As the boy tried to figure out what had gone wrong his mother took him to talk to a scientist from a local college. He learned that the butterfly was SUPPOSED to struggle. In fact, the butterfly's struggle to push its way through the tiny opening of the cocoon pushes the fluid out of its body and into its wings. Without the struggle, the butterfly would never, ever fly. The boy's good intentions had hurt the butterfly.

As you go through school, and life, keep in mind that struggling is an important part of any growth experience. In fact, it is the struggle that causes you to develop your ability to fly. [12]

The problem was that the butterfly had to build up the strength and fortitude to eventually free itself and until then it was not ready, it was out of season. If it is helped, like in the case of the child, it comes out prematurely and eventually dies. If the butterfly comes out too soon, or too

[12] http://instructor.mstc.edu/instructor/swallerm/ Struggle%20-%20Butterfly.htm

late, it will die, it must come out just at the right moment, just at the right time, when it's in its season.

Although the child had good intentions and was even compassionate and sincere, the child was wrong. I don't blame the child because he didn't know any better. However, his actions cost the butterfly to be deformed, since it was out of season. It was premature. When you are exposed to something that was meant to promote your growth, for your good and take you to higher level too soon, it could be detrimental to your life if you prematurely abort that struggle.

TRUSTING GOD FOR YOUR PARTNER

The first deficiency God realized in man is that it was not good for man to be alone. It is God who knows first what you need, when you need it. So that means if God realized it, Adam must have too, we know that by the fact that the Bible tells us he was searching, but he could not find someone comparable or compatible. Adam was not just searching for a wife he was searching for a family; therefore, to some extent, we also have that wired in our DNA, we were made for relationships, with God and with each other. If we grow up without a family, or are raised by a bad one it leaves us with deep wounds and scars that have us questioning, "was I ever good enough?" "Am I good enough?"

We frantically rush into romantic relationships without having asked God, "is this right for now?""Is this the will you have for me at this present moment of my life?" Without being patient and waiting on His approval, and trusting in God for our partner, when the romantic relationship does fail we turn around and blame God and each other. We can never change what happens with regard to failed romantic relationships if we continue trying to use the same approach.

> How many times have you perhaps been spurred on or pressured by people trying to set you up for a date? Though they might have good intentions, it could be premature just like the butterfly story.

Perhaps you have not been patient or trusted in God's perfect timing and gone online and searched for someone, who would be a suitable match? I don't believe in a match made online but I believe in a match made in heaven, chosen by God, tailored to suit and match who you are, to be compatible. I am not questioning the fact that you cannot meet the girl whom God has destined for you online, because many have found their mate that way and it has truly been a beautiful story, but let's question our motives and not be caught up with trivial matters such as the methods.

Don't allow yourself to be pushed, or pressured by people around you. Unless it's God's time, the season has not come so be patient, trust me it is worth the wait. We constantly look at other people and we start desiring and maybe even envy what they have and we then try to rationalize and justify why we should be in a relationship too; unaware that they may be already in their season for companionship, or much worse not in their season and it will eventually come to a plummeting end!

God's will for you is the dream, the promise He has in mind for your life. Some promises God has positioned and placed at a certain stations, a season that God wants you to be in, in order to receive them. No matter how much you fail or fall, it will stay there. It will not come any closer because you decided to compromise and give in to your desires and pleasure, and it won't move backwards either, it will just remain there waiting for you. God knows if you have it too soon it might destroy you and you would crack under pressure, or it might even take you away from His will and cause you to backslide.

Until you have matured and grown enough to be ushered into that season, it is not just God's will, but God's choice for you. We do not find a mate apart from God making provision for us to find one. He reveals the right partner under the right circumstances yet it is our decision, our prerogative whether we will take the person of our choice or of God's selection, not forgetting God knows best, and His selection will always be better than the selection of our choice. **He truly is Jehovah-Jira our provider, you should therefore learn to trust God for your future partner. Pray that it would not be out of season but on His time and terms, so that you will be in season.**

I like the fact that God didn't present Adam with His wife while He was still busy creating the world - no, the woman was His last creation. **When God has worked out and prepared you both on your own; where you have discovered who you are, your identity and purpose; when you have picked up the broken and shattered pieces of your life, forgiven, exhaled, gotten your priorities straight and been purged and processed, then He will say, "Son, daughter I think it is time that you start opening yourself up for that possibility…" And like the butterfly finally emerging from its cocoon, you spread out your wings and fly! It won't be too soon, it won't be too late, timing is critical; therefore it will happen just exactly when God has planned it to. It will be magical, beautiful, in season and perfect!**

He will bring you together when everything is done just as He did with creation, so that the marriage, your ceremony takes centre stage. How much God values you and marriage that He would save it for last! If God takes so much time, in so much detail, taking so much care to make sure everything is just right for the ceremony, for a family, don't you think you should too?

REASONING IN OUR SEASONING

The subtitle of this book is from Song of Songs, *Do not stir up or awaken love until the appropriate time* (Songs of Solomon 8:4HCSB) A solemn warning that should not be taken lightly. In other words do not get into a romantic relationship, unless it's your season.

In the Biblical book of Ecclesiastes chapter 3 the wise King Solomon speaks about seasons and time. *There is a time to embrace and a time to refrain from embracing and also He makes everything beautiful in its time*...**What a beautiful promise of His blessed assurance to hold onto, leading us to understand that we don't need to panic or fear, for God is working everything out for us at this very present moment.**

> **Because God values us so much, He doesn't want us to go into a relationship, and gain experience, through trial and error before it eventually works. Therefore He sets it all up, a little bit of this, a dash of that, with a pinch of salt. The Master Chef, the Master Cook mixes together the perfect stew, until you have been simmered and become exactly how He wants you to be for companionship.**

That's why God often extends our period of singleness so that more reasoning and seasoning may occur. So the next time when the pressure of life starts to intensify and people ask you, "Why are you still single?" You look up and smile, then you tell them boldly and confidently "He is not done with me yet…"

Understanding this then causes us to begin to reason more in our time of seasoning, so that God may expose, equip and empower us for living successfully as singles and for companionship. I like what Bishop T. D Jakes says, "*you made a permanent decision based on poor information and have not been exposed to better options, and you cannot make a smart decision if you have been under exposed, you cannot make great decisions with your life when you have been poorly exposed.*" Many people believe what they are experiencing at this current moment is the best that God has for them at hand and, as a result, they want to indulge, and experience it right away. Thus the statement still echoes of what I said in the introduction, *that we are the now generation, the instant generation, instant that and instant this.* We were told and learned right from the start if anything is good, it is to be enjoyed right away, or otherwise you may lose it.

This kind of thinking is the thinking that has one more dependent on self, rather than trusting and believing God has our best at heart. This selfish action has resulted in chaos and confusion. God is not the author of confusion. He is a God of order and progression, a God that set out seasons and times.

A lot of questions and perplexities occupy our mind when we start to reason in our seasoning. You perhaps want to get married because you want to get right with God, and escape the guilt of fornication. Alternatively, a lot of people want to get into a relationship and marry because they are in love with the idea of being married. Some want to get married because of age, their biological clock is ticking. Others want to get married because they want to have kids, in essence they want to get married for all the wrong reasons but have they considered whether or not it is their season? Dear son and daughter, I implore you to take time for reasoning in your seasoning.

WHEN WILL IT EVER BE MY SEASON?

I believe it is not length of time that determines the proximity of any relationship but rather depth of time. "Are you ready to be a husband or wife?" What we should be really asking here is, "Are you ready within your life?"

You see, anytime you have allowed God to take you through your personal process and then usher you into this season where He says, "now my son, daughter"-that's your 'in season'. It would be like what Adam and Eve had, we have no record of them ever splitting or divorcing. It would be like a Ruth finding her Boaz or an Esther who, although she found favour in the sight of the king, had to go through 12 months of preparation before she was ready, her 'in season'.

There will never be a good time for a romantic relationship unless it is the right time. The right time is God's time. When it's God's time you are in season; when it is not, you are out of season. One of the first pre-requisites in understanding when it is the right time for a relationship is to realize God's purpose for us first. He has a work for us as individuals first, a plan for our own individual lives.

"Then the Lord God took the man and put him in the Garden of Eden to work it and keep it." (Genesis 2v15) *And God blessed them. And God said to them, "Be fruitful and multiply and fill the earth and subdue it and have dominion over the fish of the sea and over the birds of the heavens and over every living thing that moves on earth."* (Genesis 1v28) *"The man gave names to all the livestock and to all the birds of the heavens and to every beast of the field."* (Genesis 2v20) Our purpose is defined in the expression of God's will for our lives.

Ever since the fall of humanity, we became feeble, fragile and imperfect human beings. As a result our relationships are set in imperfection. The only perfection we have is what God imparts through His Son. We sanctify our partners with the Word. As iron sharpens iron so will one partner shape the countenance of another. Thus the right time and season is when two people with the right spirit and attitude are yoked together.

The whole aim of scripture is to teach us about a God that wants to have a relationship with us, an undeserving people. The Word demonstrates the extent to which He went to make the relationship possible. Only when one is able to respond appropriately to this relationship will he/she be able to succeed in companionship. As God accepts and loves us with all our shortcomings, so we need to respond in our relationships. When you have captured this spirit, and you are able to carry it into the relationship, then you are ready.

Note it is not perfection of performance that makes good relationships, but the Spirit of God.

SAMANTHA

BECAUSE I'M SINGLE

I am not consciously choosing to stay single indefinitely, for I have a deep desire to meet up with my Adam one day, when it's the right time and season.

That said however, I chose not to settle, I chose not to compromise, I chose to wait patiently and sometimes impatiently upon the Lord, for joining myself to another is the second most important decision I will make in this lifetime, the first being accepting Christ as my Saviour of course.

My past relationships were all while I was still unsaved. There were two relationships that still stand out in my memory, because of the intensity of the love, or what I thought was love at that time; I didn't know what love was then. I only had one other romantic relationship since accepting Christ as my Saviour, and because we met in church I automatically assumed that the guy was sent from God.

I remember our first encounter when we were at church and it was time for the offerings basket to be passed around. He sat three chairs down from me, and while I was still scrambling in my bag for some pennies, he suddenly reached over and folded a R50 note in my hand. I was taken aback and looked at him quizzically... to which he simply replied "I want God to bless you more". That introduction set the tone for everything that was to come, and when times were tough in the relationship, I always remembered his obedience to the Holy Spirit and his willingness to help others.

Yet we failed miserably at making the relationship work. Although we wanted to honour God's command and not have sex before marriage, we danced around the fire of temptation, seeing the cliff up ahead that would lead to ruin, and thought we were able and strong enough not to give way to the fire that was eating us up. God sent many warning signs at that time - dreams, a word spoken and His voice saying we should flee this temptation, but we continued to cuddle, kiss and touch just enough to arouse more desires. In our mind, we were not contravening God's commands, as we still had not had 'sex' yet, no penetration, no actual physical intercourse that would warrant fornication we thought. Until we finally went too far, the way I fell pregnant was very odd, and I won't trouble you with all the details, but we were fools, we played with fire and got badly burned, that's the short of it.

The relationship fell to pieces and we broke up, although we got engaged and were on the verge of getting married, for all the wrong reasons of course. We just could not agree on so many things. I realized that the guy was not what I wanted; he was the exact opposite of what I wanted.

I wanted a man who would fear God and not be willing to take any shortcuts; I wanted a man who would lead by example and help me not to give in to temptation; I wanted a man who would be saturated in the Word such that it would lead him so that he could guard me as Christ guards the church. I wanted a man who had compassion and vigour for God and His Kingdom; I wanted a man who would put God first in all things and all areas of his life. I wanted a man who was seeking holiness as God ask us to be Holy for He is Holy.

I wanted a Joshua who would say, for me and my house we will serve the Lord. An Abraham who would accept by faith what God promises even if there is nothing to prove it, so it would be credited to him as righteousness. I wanted a humble Moses who would lead his people to God; a David who would please God and even when he sins, confesses to God and still seeks His face.

I wanted a MAN OF GOD!

Because I am single,

I will wait for a MAN OF GOD who will guard me and be the priest in my house.

Because I am single, I will believe that God has a plan and a purpose for my life, to prosper me, to give me a hope.

What no eye has seen, what no ear has heard, that's how incredible the future is that awaits me.

Because I am single, I will not fear loneliness for He has not given me a spirit of fear, but a spirit of power, love and a sound mind.

Because I am single, I will use this time to prepare my heart, my mind and my body for my husband, so that he will find me whole.

I will be his helpmate, his cheerleader, his friend and his companion.

I will be a blessing unto him, for God has prepared me to walk alongside him.

Because I am single, I will use this time to bury all my past hurts and disappointments,

The disillusionment of broken relationships, the lies that struck a chord in my heart, and the promises that were never kept by so many,

All these I will leave behind me, so that I don't punish my husband for somebody else's mistake,

So that I will give him all of me, a complete heart that will love and cherish him.

I will encourage and defend him,

I will believe that he is able to do all things through Christ who strengthens him.

I will be the original Eve that God designed before the fall of man,

And he will be the original Adam that God designed to have dominion and rule over the earth.

We will be exactly what God intended marriage to be. Two becoming ONE.

"How lovely, how pure, how absolutely beautiful to have waited and kept yourself till you married…"

Samantha is single and she trusts that God will usher her into that season of companionship, when she will be good and ready…

Getting into a relationship now would be great, with marriage being the goal. Don't get caught up doing the right thing, at the wrong time, with the wrong people, hoping for the right outcome, however.

To my future wife to be

While I am having fun, chasing dreams, setting new goals and remaining focused and purposely driven,

I am patient with the process,

I understand that our discovery of who we are in Him first, will eventually lead to the discovery of each other

I have allowed God to be the author and finisher of our love story. I will wait for you, but

Don't catch me out of season...

If you loved reading El-Roy R. Cook's debut book *Because I'm Single*, you'll love his next book to follow *Vision: The Pathway to Your Dream*. Here's the introduction to the book.

VISION: THE PATHWAY TO DREAM
YOUR

INTRODUCTION

There is a treasure worth more than silver, rubies, diamonds and gold. Some would call it one of life's greatest commodities; the highest accolade life could bestow on anyone; the fusion of one's preparation and purpose culminating in the ultimate promise. However, in the lives of people everywhere its scarcity dims the light of whether or not it could even be attainable. People from all walks of life, no matter what their creed, conduct or belief; the brave, the feeble and insecure; the rich and the poor, the known and forgotten, have all sought it, some even fought and died for it. It's what ignites our passion, gives rise to our imagination and causes us to cross the boundaries of perceived limitations; to venture, explore and conquer, all for its realization - our Dream.

Whether you dream of driving a smart car, owning a big house on the top of a hill or on a beach-front with the ocean as your front yard, your garden enchanting and magical, or perhaps you dream of publishing that book that you always said you would, with the hopes of it being a best seller. Perhaps you dream of producing music that hits the top of the charts and goes gold and on to platinum. Perhaps you dream of finishing school, eventually obtaining your diploma, degree or PhD; or you dream of acting, landing that major deal where you're a star in the leading role. Do you dream of starting up your own business, becoming CEO, pioneering and inventing something new? Or do you dream of making it to the national team, competing in the Olympics representing your country with pride, with the cherry on top achieving the gold medal, the pinnacle of your career? Do you dream of that day when you finally get to walk down the aisle with your Mr. or Mrs. Right, starting a family of your own and living happily ever after? We dream of a better country, nation and world, where we will truly be our brothers' and sisters' keepers; we dream of a better life and a brighter tomorrow. We dream about a lot of things and whatever those dreams may be, our dreams come in all shapes, sizes and forms. When one dream has been realized, the focus then starts to shift…

Our dream is what beckons us, the fire that burns deep within our heart, each step we take, each move we make and with every breath we take. With boldness, confidence, excitement and enthusiasm we cannot wait to share our dreams and follow the path in relentless pursuit of them. Exhausting our effort, we would dare stand up to face our fears without hesitation or so much as flinching. No mountain would be high enough, no struggle hard enough and no storm strong enough for the forces and factors that drive us for the sake of realizing our dreams. Many would give up all of the treasures of this world just to possess it!

We have a lot of dreamers but sadly few people possess the vision it requires to make their dreams a reality; they question themselves about their possibility. The twinkle in their eyes fades; they give up trying and give up rising altogether as they allow their aspirations, potential and dreams to subside into a world of the unrealized and untapped, locked away forever fading away into the corridors of time passed.

I often find myself drifting in day-dreams. In my dreams I am without restriction, limitation or boundary, where the sky is not even near to the limit of what my mind's eye sees is possible. I lay a firm foundation and I am the architect of my own Utopia. There is an abundance of resources all around; it's the most fertile place anyone could find, colourful, beautiful and opulent; flowers freshly blossomed; birds are singing, the air is pungent with flavours and fragrances; a sight that would woo you. I construct and reconstruct as I see fit. The unreachable becomes so much more reachable, the impossible becomes possible. I can be superman soaring and gliding through the sky like an eagle or 007 on my next top secret mission. It's in that moment one could say, that I have captured a picture perfect moment that is indescribable and mesmerizing.

It's a bright sunny day, clear blue skies with no cloud in sight. There is joy and laughter all around, family and friends have gathered as I present my mom the keys to her brand new house, "Mom here's the house I always promised I would buy for you..." She is overwhelmed with emotion, tears of joy run down her face; I embrace her in a hug. You can hear the clinging of champagne glasses as we toast to this momentous occasion.

The next scene I am at my own house, my family has come over as I give them a tour of the house I always dreamed about that now finally I own.

The dining room is separated by two glass, sliding doors from the living room, the kind of sliding doors that you find at a mall that opens when a sensor senses someone's presence. In the lounge, framed portraits are on the wall and books are packed neatly on shelves with the most exquisite sofas standing nearby. An old antique theme could best describe this room; in this lounge is a sparkling, grand piano with black-pearl finish, it is the arresting piece in the room. A beautifully framed picture of me, my wife and kids stands on top of it. It captures a relative's attention. "Remember the grand piano I always told you I would have in my house El-Ton? Well this is it!" I exclaim. They share how proud and happy they are because of what I have become and achieved, as we carry on with the rest of the tour. I am taken back and forward to different scenes of, let's call it, my Dream World.

The place is filled to the brim with people, music playing softly in the background as I sign some books and also take a few photos with guests, followed by this event at last being opened, and the public reading of the first chapter of my book as I also explain a little bit about my journey. It's been a long hard, trying road, but I have made it. I thank everyone for their presence, those who assisted, advised and helped in any way and mostly God who by His grace has kept and sustained me through all these years and has made all of this possible. It still feels a bit unreal, but it's the launch of my book. My long-time dream has become a reality.

I have a collection of cars, a Lamborghini and Ferrari just to name a few. I am married to the most beautiful wife, inside and out, with kids who are my bundle of joy and I feel like the happiest man alive. I have travelled all over the world, stood and fought for a cause greater than my own and have become a household name and my rise has been slow but sure.

Suddenly, as I snap out of it I am right back to where I started and it dawns on me that life feels dull and boring with the same mundane routine. There is no adventure and no excitement. It has just been another day-dream and the harshness of reality sets in…

How many of you can relate? We often find ourselves day-dreaming about losing weight, getting in shape and even winning the lottery. We dream of promotion, obtaining that degree, diploma or doctorate whatever. Sadly, it is all it ever amounts to; that's where it stays…

Have you really asked yourself this question, "What separates dreamers from achievers?" Well this vital factor is not aptitude, heredity, lack of money or resources really, but lack of Vision.

That is why the poorest man alive is not the man without any money, but the man without a vision for his life. Vision comprises the calculated and strategic actions taken in response to your life's purpose. Vision is the roadmap to your destination and the pathway to your dream. You say that you have big dreams; I ask you, whether or not your vision is big enough to meet the demand of your dream? Vision sees the detail and meets the demand of your dream; for no builder builds without counting the cost first. Your dream will cost you nothing, but having vision will cost you blood, sweat and tears and cause you to move beyond the threshold of some of your disappointments and fears. Vision therefore requires the execution of a carefully plotted plan.

Vision is indeed that underlying factor, the key to ushering you through the pathway to your Dream. So, if ever you have the hopes of realizing your dreams, you have to realize vision is not only essential, but necessary. Hence, it is imperative to possess the kind of vision that will enable you to access and attain your dreams. To enlarge your vision, so that you will be provoked to go to the next level, where your dreams becomes a tangible reality; this book is without a doubt a must read!

REFERENCES

Chapter 1

Harris, J. 1997, 2003. *I Kissed Dating Goodbye*. United States of America: Multnomah Books

Chapter 2

Munroe, Dr. M. 2005. *The Spirit of Leadership*. United States of America: Whitaker House

Enterprise, T.D.J. *Before You Do*. Copyright © 2008. United States of America: Atria Books

Zacharias, R. 2004. *I, Isaac, Take Thee, Rebekah*. United States of America: W Publishing Group, a Division of Thomas Nelson, Inc.

James 1:8

Chapter 3

Jakes, T.D. 1995. *Loose That Man & Let Him Go!* United States of America: Bethany House Publisher

Jakes, T.D. 1995. *Loose That Man & Let Him Go!* United States of America: Bethany House Publisher

Chapter 4

http://en.m.wikipedia.org/wiki/Psychological_trauma

Jakes, T.D. 1995.*Loose That Man & Let Him Go!* United States of America: Bethany House Publisher

Chapter 5

http://www.naijapicks.com/2012/12/a-true-life-story-written-by-college.html

Chapter 6

Washer, P. and Washer, C. January 1998. *The Godly Woman, Becoming Esther.* HeartCry magazine Volume 3. ©

http://www.TheButterFlySite.com

Chapter 7

http://instructor.mstc.edu/instructor/swallerm/Struggle%20-%20Butterfly.htm

Munroe, Dr. M. 2005. *The Spirit of Leadership.* United States of America: Whitaker House

www.ingramcontent.com/pod-product-compliance
Lightning Source LLC
Chambersburg PA
CBHW061822040426
42447CB00012B/2768